Second Corinthians

INTERPRETATION
A Bible Commentary for Teaching and Preaching

INTERPRETATION
A BIBLE COMMENTARY FOR TEACHING AND PREACHING

James Luther Mays, *Editor*
Patrick D. Miller, Jr., *Old Testament Editor*
Paul J. Achtemeier, *New Testament Editor*

ERNEST BEST

Second Corinthians

INTERPRETATION

A Bible Commentary
for Teaching and Preaching

John Knox Press
ATLANTA

Library of Congress Cataloging-in-Publication Data

Best, Ernest.
    Second Corinthians.

    (Interpretation, a Bible commentary for teaching and
preaching)
    Bibliography: p.
    1. Bible. N.T. Corinthians, 2nd—Commentaries.
I. Title.   II. Series.
BS2675.3.B47   1987   227′.307   86-45404
ISBN 0-8042-3135-4

© copyright John Knox Press 1987
10 9 8 7 6 5 4 3 2 1
Printed in the United States of America
John Knox Press
Atlanta, Georgia 30365

SERIES PREFACE

This series of commentaries offers an interpretation of the books of the Bible. It is designed to meet the need of students, teachers, ministers, and priests for a contemporary expository commentary. These volumes will not replace the historical critical commentary or homiletical aids to preaching. The purpose of this series is rather to provide a third kind of resource, a commentary which presents the integrated result of historical and theological work with the biblical text.

An interpretation in the full sense of the term involves a text, an interpreter, and someone for whom the interpretation is made. Here, the text is what stands written in the Bible in its full identity as literature from the time of "the prophets and apostles," the literature which is read to inform, inspire, and guide the life of faith. The interpreters are scholars who seek to create an interpretation which is both faithful to the text and useful to the church. The series is written for those who teach, preach, and study the Bible in the community of faith.

The comment generally takes the form of expository essays. It is planned and written in the light of the needs and questions which arise in the use of the Bible as Holy Scripture. The insights and results of contemporary scholarly research are used for the sake of the exposition. The commentators write as exegetes and theologians. The task which they undertake is both to deal with what the texts say and to discern their meaning for faith and life. The exposition is the unified work of one interpreter.

The text on which the comment is based is the Revised Standard Version of the Bible. The general availability of this translation makes the printing of a translation unnecessary and saves the space for comment. The text is divided into sections appropriate to the particular book; comment deals with passages as a whole, rather than proceeding word by word, or verse by verse.

Writers have planned their volumes in light of the requirements set by the exposition of the book assigned to them. Biblical books differ in character, content, and arrangement. They also differ in the way they have been and are used in the liturgy, thought, and devotion of the church. The distinctiveness and use of particular books have been taken into account in decisions about the approach, emphasis, and use of space in the commentaries. The goal has been to allow writers to develop the format which provides for the best presentation of their interpretation.

The result, writers and editors hope, is a commentary which both explains and applies, an interpretation which deals with both the meaning and the significance of biblical texts. Each commentary reflects, of course, the writer's own approach and perception of the church and world. It could and should not be otherwise. Every interpretation of any kind is individual in that sense; it is one reading of the text. But all who work at the interpretation of Scripture in the church need the help and stimulation of a colleague's reading and understanding of the text. If these volumes serve and encourage interpretation in that way, their preparation and publication will realize their purpose.

The Editors

Preface

I wish to express my thanks to the editors of this series for their invitation to write on Second Corinthians. This was a special pleasure to me since one of the great commentaries on that letter from a past age was that in *The Expositor's Bible* by James Denney, a former Principal and Professor of New Testament in Trinity College, Glasgow. Since his days this college has been united with the Faculty of Divinity in the University of Glasgow, and as Professor of Divinity and Biblical Criticism there I became in a sense his successor. I have no expectation however that my commentary will be as penetrating and profound as was his in its day.

I wish also to thank the editors for their continual helpful comments on the way this commentary should go. They are not responsible for any of it but without their wise guidance it would have been much less suited to its purpose. My thanks are also due to the Librarian, Beth Nichol, of Knox College, Dunedin, New Zealand, and her staff. Since a large part of the first draft of my work was written there when separated from my own books, their assistance was invaluable.

Ernest Best

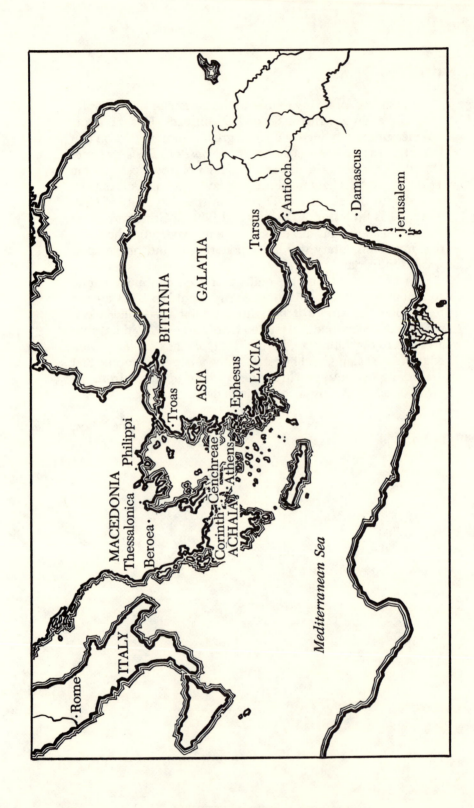

CONTENTS

x

Introduction

Although Corinth was an ancient Greek city, it had been totally destroyed by the Romans in 146 B.C., and the site lay unused for about a hundred years. It was then rebuilt by Julius Caesar as a Roman city and became the seat of government of the Roman province of Achaia. Like most major cities of the ancient world it contained a considerable number of Jews. It was among these that Paul, in accordance with his normal practice, began his mission (Acts 18:4). Corinth is often described as an exceptionally licentious city, but most of the evidence for this relates to the earlier Greek city and not to the Roman. In Paul's day it was probably no worse or no better than any large cosmopolitan area. While some passages in First Corinthians refer to its sexual immorality, this is not an important factor in Second Corinthians. What Paul writes in this letter has little to do with immediate local and external circumstances but much with the internal life of the Christian community in Corinth.

For fuller information about Corinth and its history see articles in Bible dictionaries under "Corinth" and the introductions to the commentaries listed in the Bibliography.

By the time Paul wrote Second Corinthians he had been deeply concerned with the church there for a number of years. His first visit, when he evangelized the city, lasted more than eighteen months (Acts 18:11). After leaving to continue his mission in other areas, he wrote back on several occasions. Not all of this has survived. I Corinthians 5:9–11 shows that even prior to that letter (our First Corinthians), he had already written to Corinth. He wrote First Corinthians because of information he received from "Chloe's people" (I Cor. 1:11), who for some reason had traveled from Corinth to Ephesus where Paul was. The Corinthians themselves had also written seeking his advice on problems facing them (I Cor. 7:1). In I Corinthians 4:18–21 he said he hoped to visit Corinth again in the near future. He later changed this intention, planning instead to visit it twice

1

(II Cor. 1:15–16), once on his way from Ephesus to Macedonia and again on his way back to Ephesus. He never made this double visit and was accused of indecision (II Cor. 1:17; see comment on 1:15–22). However he did pay a single visit (II Cor. 13:2; 2:1). It was not a happy occasion either for him or for the Corinthians. After it he wrote a strong and angry letter (see II Cor. 2:3). This is variously known as the intermediate, severe, painful, or tearful letter. It is not our Second Corinthians. This came later, though not necessarily all at once (it may be an amalgam of letters). While he was writing these various letters and visiting Corinth, his assistants were also going back and forth there. See I Corinthians 16:10 and II Corinthians 2:13; 7:6–7 for visits by Timothy and Titus. In II Corinthians 8:16–24 Paul says he will send Titus and two others to Corinth. These visits and the writing of all the letters took place within five or six years of his original mission to the city.

It is not possible to fix Paul's visits and those of his associates to Corinth into a rigid scheme with his letters for there are considerable doubts whether our Second Corinthians is a single letter. It may consist of portions of several letters of Paul which someone at Corinth put together after his death in order to preserve them. Anyone reading the letter carefully is aware of a break of thought after 2:13 and finds that the theme of 1:3—2:13 is picked up again at 7:5 and continued through the remainder of chapter 7. Within 2:14 to 7:4 the brief passage 6:14—7:1 again breaks the sequence of thought. From 2:14 to 7:4 (without 6:14—7:1) may then be part of a separate letter. Chapters 8 and 9, while dealing with the same issue, the collection for the poor saints in Jerusalem, treat the matter differently and may also have originally formed sections in different letters. There is a very clear break both in thought and in mood at the end of Chapter 9, and a very strong case can be made for regarding the whole of chapters 10—13 as coming from another letter. Many scholars identify this with the intermediate or painful letter. More probably chapters 10—13 come from a letter written after chapters 1—9. If so, they depict another stage in which relations between Paul and the Corinthians again became worse after the improvement indicated in 7:5–16. This deterioration was caused by preachers who came into Corinth from other Christian communities with ideas about Jesus and the gospel which were very different from those of Paul. Because of this he therefore says in 12:14 and 13:2

2

that he may need to make yet another visit. If chapters 10—13 are an integral part of Second Corinthians or if they form part of an independent but later letter we do not know the final outcome of Paul's relations with the Corinthians (see Conclusion for brief discussion). Detailed outlines with evaluation of the suggested division of Second Corinthians into separate letters or portions from separate letters will be found both in the introductory sections of the commentaries listed in the Bibliography and in the sections on the Corinthian correspondence in New Testament introductions.

Fortunately our understanding of what Paul was saying to the Corinthians does not depend on a full and final solution to all the critical questions concerning the number of letters, or parts of letters, incorporated in our Second Corinthians. Some areas remain obscure, and will always do so, but by and large we can see what he was getting at as he wrote to this very troublesome church. It is also fortunate that the paragraphs into which we tend to divide the letter for lectionary and teaching purposes rarely overlap possible divisions between letters. If then we take it a paragraph at a time, we are probably dealing in that paragraph with the same letter.

Second Corinthians, or its various constituents, is much more concerned with what is happening inside the church than with the relation of its members to the world outside. The only real exception is 6:14—7:1. Saying that the letter is concerned with what is happening within the church should not be taken as limiting its concern to Corinth. The church exists in other areas as well as in Corinth. When Paul writes about the collection to be sent to Jerusalem (chapters 8, 9), he has in mind the church there and the churches in Macedonia as well as the church in Corinth.

Tensions can blow up within an individual congregation left to itself because members have never fully shaken off the ways of life and thought of their pre-Christian period. Some may hold on to these more firmly than others. Tensions can also be brought about by outside circumstances, for example, persecution. How are the faithful to treat those who have not stood as firmly as themselves? Finally tensions can be created when Christians from other churches with differing ideas about the gospel come into the community. This is particularly so if they attack the existing views of the community or its founder. This is what happened in Corinth.

3

INTERPRETATION

Because Second Corinthians is so much taken up with the internal life of the community and Paul's relations with it, we learn much more about Paul himself from it than from any other of his letters. We may not learn simple facts like his age or appearance, but we see him responding to many different situations and so understand better the kind of person he was. We meet the human Paul rather than the Paul of Christian legend and piety. If there are times when he seems to fall short of what we expect, we should remember that he faced terrible strains including the possibility of a partial or total failure of his work in Corinth. No one has ever claimed that Paul was without fault or sinless. If there are blemishes in his character, nothing is to be gained by concealing them. We can even learn from them.

Because of the nature of the letter we also learn a great deal about how pastoral responsibility should be exercised. George Herbert, in one of the great spiritual classics of the English language, *The Country Parson,* wrote

> What an admirable Epistle is the second to the *Corinthians?* how full of affections? he (i.e. Paul) joys, and he is sorry, he grieves, and he glories, never was there such care of a flock expressed, save in the great shepherd of the fold, who first shed tears over *Jerusalem,* and afterwards blood (p. 63).

Paul's pastoral position was probably unique, but all Christians are in some kind of a pastoral situation in relation to others, as parents, teachers, administrators, executives, supervisors, as working alongside others and in constant contact with them. All are the keepers of their brothers and sisters. How then should they care for them? All Christians are also subject to some kind of pastoral responsibility exercised over them by others. What should their attitude be to those who exercise that responsibility? How do they decide between those competing for their obedience? This letter is then especially helpful to all Christians, and it is to be assumed throughout this commentary that when the words "pastor" and "pastoral" are used they apply to all Christians and not just to ministers and priests unless the latter application is made specifically clear.

As we read through our letter we should remember that letters are one of the easiest ways of unintentionally concealing information. Writer and readers share a knowledge about what is going on that the reader from outside their circle who chances on the letter does not possess. This is especially true of a letter which deals with the inner situation of a group. Its members know the situation and do not need to have it recalled to them. We need not then expect to be able to understand all that Paul writes. As we read through our letter we shall repeatedly find that there are issues which we cannot grasp fully because we are so far removed from the situation of writer and readers. We can however usually see enough to gain some insight into the way we should exercise our pastoral responsibilities, and accept the pastoral care others offer to us, and into the way we should expect the Christian communities to which we belong to behave.

If nothing else, Second Corinthians demonstrates to us the variety of views within the New Testament church. That church was not a group of impeccable saints but one of sinners in the process of being saved and of thinking through the meaning of their faith. If they were to be saved and understand their faith, they needed wise guidance and Paul gives them this. Though our situations may be very different, his counsel may also assist us in our Christian lives. The letter is valuable to us in another way, for despite its seeming occupation with disputes over matters apparently remote from us, every now and then it blossoms out into profound theology, a theology arising out of and shaped by the concrete situation (e.g., 1:3–11; 1:19–20; 4:7–12; 5:1–10; 5:14–21; 8:9; 12:9,10). Paul cast everything about which he wrote and thought into theological terms and was therefore continually driven back to express himself in basic Christian ways. From these basic positions we are able to move forward again to our own particular problems.

But how do we move forward from the longer and more pastoral sections? We can begin by applying them to ourselves, for we are all pastors of some kind. If we are preachers, we can apply them to the "pastors" in our congregations. The nature of such "pastorates" varies greatly from congregation to congregation, but there will always be parents. For this reason some attention has been paid throughout to parental pastoral responsibility. Because however of the intimate and varied nature of pastoral care, there are few direct "applications" of pastoral passages with suggestions as to how they might be preached. The application or actualization of the text lies in its very exposition, in the questions it poses whether deliberately drawn out or not. We are "Paul" or we are the "Corinthians"

5

or we are (God forbid) "the opponents." From the letter we thus learn basic attitudes to pastoral care rather than techniques and ways to deal with particular situations. Few, indeed, of the standard and recurring pastoral situations (e.g., bereavement, preparation for marriage, single parent families) are treated in this letter.

At a number of points in the commentary there are included general sections on wider aspects of some of the subjects which Paul treats. These general sections should always be read when any paragraph to which they apply is being considered. Thus if you are interested in any portion of chapters 8 and 9 on the collection you should always read the "Introduction" and the "Concluding Remarks."

Readers who do not know Greek and consult translations other than the Revised Standard Version will observe that these do not always agree in detail with it (the RSV). In most cases there is much to be said for and against different translations. In this commentary we have tended to remain with the Revised Standard Version without discussion. Rarely, if ever, is the main thought of the passage affected. In commenting we have also normally followed the paragraphing of that translation (RSV).

PART ONE

Paul Deals
with the Past

II CORINTHIANS 1:1—2:13

II Corinthians 1:1–2
Address

Paul used the same form for his letters as everyone else in the ancient world, and so he begins by identifying himself as the writer and the Corinthians as the recipients. He then greets them (1:1–2) and follows this with a thanksgiving or blessing (1:3–11) which leads into the main section of the letter. The length of none of these items in letters was fixed, and Paul is never content with the barest minimum. A glance at his other letters shows the elements which are common to all and those which are peculiar to each. The variations arise out of the particular circumstances of each church. One difficulty in understanding the address and blessing of Second Corinthians comes because this letter may be a combination of several letters, but the address and blessing will have applied to only one of them. (On the possibility of the combination of several letters in our letter see Introduction.)

In identifying himself Paul says he is "an apostle of Christ Jesus by the will of God." He had not appointed himself to be an apostle (see Gal. 1:1, 11–17). God had chosen him and revealed Christ to him as he traveled to Damascus (Acts 9:1–9). Because of this he regards himself as an apostle on a par with those like Peter, whom Jesus chose while on earth. Like them he had seen the Lord (I Cor. 9:1). On the meaning of "apostle" see further on 11:5,13; 12:11–12. As an apostle Paul has been given a special commission to take the gospel to the Gentiles

7

(Rom. 11:13), and what he says, writes, and does carries the authority of Jesus who appointed him. Second Corinthians is not then the letter of a private individual to a group of friends but a letter carrying divine authority. In his writing as in all he did Paul was given tremendous confidence by his belief that he had been appointed to act in the name of Christ. But, as he writes, the situation in Corinth had become difficult. His position as an apostle had been challenged. This begins to appear in 2:1–11; 7:2–13 and becomes a main theme in chapters 10—13. So at the outset he reminds them of his apostleship.

In the address he associates with himself Timothy who was one of his regular helpers and who was known to the Corinthians. Timothy had been with Paul during part of Paul's initial mission (Acts 18:5; II Cor. 1:19) and had returned since then at least once to Corinth (I Cor. 4:17; 16:10–11).

Paul addresses both the church which he had founded in Corinth and "all the saints who are in the whole of Achaia" (see a map). Corinth was the capital of the Roman province of Achaia. Achaia contained Athens but not Beroea, Thessalonica and Philippi, which were in Macedonia. Though Athens was the more renowned city in Achaia, Corinth contained the chief church. There would probably also have been pockets of Christians in other towns in the area (e.g., Cenchreae, see Rom. 16:1). These would have been evangelized from Corinth. Since Paul speaks of "saints" and not of "churches," they may not have been organized into regular congregations. Paul invariably uses "saints" in the plural, for Christians are never isolated individuals but always part of a community, the church. "Saints" are not Christians who are especially good; all Christians are saints, that is, "holy" (the Greek is the same), because God has brought them into his holy people. They belong to God. This should give them the same confidence in all that they do as Paul had from his belief that God had appointed him.

The address ends with a greeting. The normal greeting of one Jew for another is *shalom* or "peace." It refers not to inner serenity but to the relation of a person to God. Christ's death created peace between Christians and God. Paul prays that it continue. The normal Greek greeting was *chairein*. It means little more than "good luck." Instead of using it Paul chooses a word drawn from the same Greek root but which is heavy with theological overtones: "grace." The similarity and the change would be obvious to a Greek and would come as a shock when

8

first heard. All Christian existence depends on God's grace. It denotes both the favor with which God looks on people (and why should he? they continually disappoint him) and the power he gives them to serve him. Both the peace and the grace of God are seen above all in Jesus and in the love with which he served us and died for us. Without him we would not know the full depth of God's peace and grace.

II Corinthians 1:3–11
Thanksgiving

In this passage there are two themes which cannot be entirely distinguished but need to be developed separately. The first is found in verses 3–7 and connects what Paul suffers and the comfort he receives to the sufferings of the Corinthians and the comfort they receive. The second in verses 8–11 deals with one particular occasion on which Paul suffered and with his deliverance from that suffering.

Comfort in Affliction (1:3–7)

In most of his letters after the address Paul continues with the phrase "I (we) thank God." Here instead he adopts a Jewish form of prayer beginning "Blessed be the God . . ." Christians were already probably using it at the Eucharist; see also Ephesians 1:3–14; I Peter 1:3–9. This form enables him to begin with an assertion about God and in its light to speak of his own sufferings, those of the Corinthians, and of the comfort they all receive. Paul adapts the Jewish form to Christian use by introducing Christ into it. He continues to worship the same God he had worshiped as a Jew, but now as a Christian he knows him in a new way as "the Father of our Lord Jesus Christ." Because of what God has done in and through the death and resurrection of Jesus, Paul can be more sure that he is a God who is merciful and who comforts. The keyword is "comfort," but comfort is unnecessary where there is no suffering. Thus, though Paul begins the passage with the reference to the God who comforts, we begin with the nature of the suffering to which the comfort is God's response.

9

INTERPRETATION

When we think of suffering most of us have in mind things like natural disasters or illness. Such suffering seems a matter of chance and wholly unrelated to the way we live our lives. But we also often suffer through our own past actions (lung cancer through smoking) or the actions of others (unemployment strikes in middle life because the employing firm is closed down by a holding company to magnify its profits). All these are sufferings which happen to people because they are people. If Christians experience them, they do so because they are people and not because they are Christians. The sufferings Paul has in mind on the other hand happen to Christians because they are Christians.

He mentions one particular suffering of his own (v. 8). We do not know what it was (see on vv. 8–11), but it was an experience that almost overcame his faith. Whatever it was, it came to him in the course of his mission and because of it. Acts tells us of many of the trials he experienced, and he himself lists some of them in 11:23–29. The Corinthians have also suffered, and that again because they are Christians. Paul does not describe their sufferings, but other parts of the New Testament supply glimpses of what they may have been: riots (Acts 17:5–9; 19:28–41), false accusations in court (I Peter 4:15–16), imprisonment (Heb. 13:3), homes and businesses broken up (Heb. 10: 32–34). We are helped to understand what happened when we read accounts of those who became Christians in the missionary expansion of the last one hundred and fifty years and of those who today try to remain Christian under rightwing dictatorships or in communist countries.

We talk and write about the problem of suffering. Paul never did. We ask why national and natural disasters occur, why loved ones take ill and die, why people are thrown on the scrapheap of unemployment while they have still many useful years of work ahead of them. Paul never asked such questions, nor did he become embittered by what happened to him. He knew his sufferings were unavoidable because he had no option but to follow Christ and preach him. Christ had promised nothing less to believers (Mark 8:34). But Paul also knew that every time he suffered he was comforted (v. 4), and the comfort was more wonderful than the suffering was terrifying. His suffering was a sign to him that he was truly serving Christ. Coming neither by chance nor as a divine punishment, it always brought its own consolation. Some people use suffering as an argument

10

against the existence of God; for Paul it confirmed his faith in him. Perhaps Paul thought the Corinthians were worried by their sufferings and so began his letter by referring to them, but he never treats such suffering as a problem, for he wants the Corinthians to realize the marvelous reward suffering brings in comfort.

This comfort is not the removal of suffering nor the assurance that everything will turn out all right in the end nor that others have suffered worse things nor that it will soon be over. None of these things may ever happen. What Paul does is to associate comfort with salvation (v. 6). The God of comfort is also the God of mercy (v. 3), and because he is a God of mercy he saves. When Paul describes the terrible thing that happened to him (v. 8), he calls the comfort he received "life from death" (vv. 9–10). It is not an added extra to salvation but is a part of it. What this means is not fully explained here. From what Paul writes elsewhere we can see that the comfort lies in knowing Christ better, in being more firmly united to him as risen and, thereby, to the Christian community. The point he makes here is not the nature of the comfort but the way it can be transferred from one person to another within the church.

When, then, Paul says here that he is comforted, it is not to express his self-satisfaction that God has comforted him. He affirms instead that through his sufferings and the comfort he has received the Corinthians have been comforted (v. 4). He has been afflicted and comforted for their comfort and salvation (v. 6). They have shared in his sufferings, and so they will share in his comfort.

That there is a community in suffering and comfort, those who have been involved in some great disaster will confirm. People who in their previous ordinary life paid little heed to one another suddenly find themselves helping and supporting others and being helped and supported. This happened in the blitzes on British cities in World War II. It does not take a war to produce this spirit. In Alcoholics Anonymous the members draw support from one another and are enabled to stand together, and what is that but comforting one another. There are many examples where one member of a family is born with a disability or suffers a crippling disease and the family, and perhaps even the person, set out not only to help the stricken member of that family but move outward to help others who suffer the same affliction. If Christianity is the inspiration here,

11

as it often is, we come nearer to what Paul has in mind.

He writes of himself as sharing abundantly in Christ's sufferings (v. 5). This means more than that he suffered like Christ. The Jews believed that the Messiah (i.e., Christ), when he appeared, would not suffer but that the period just prior to his arrival would be one of great suffering for those who expected him. They spoke of the birth pangs (a form of suffering) of the time of the Messiah. For Paul, the Messiah had already come, but he was coming again shortly, and he, Paul, was bearing the birth pangs of that second coming in the sufferings he endured in his mission work.

That does not exhaust everything Paul meant; if it did, it might not have any meaning for us who do not necessarily believe the Messiah is just about to return. Paul is a member of the church, the body of Christ; Christ suffered in his earthly body; suffering still belongs to his body the church. Paul shares in the suffering of that body for he suffers with Christ (Rom. 8:17); he carries in himself the death of Jesus (II Cor. 4:10); he dies every day (I Cor. 15:31). Yet also as a member of the body of Christ, Paul shares in the comfort that belongs to that body. The Corinthians too are in that body. In it if one member suffers all suffer together (I Cor. 12:26) and if one member is comforted all are comforted. So Paul in his own suffering brings comfort to the Corinthians. In the final issue Paul does not comfort them only by the example of his suffering or through his letters and sermons, though these all help. He comforts them because he and they are members of Christ's body. (For another aspect of the transference of suffering see 4:7–12).

Paul was comforted directly by God and so the Corinthians will be, and if so, Paul will be comforted by them. In this he is like any member of the body of Christ. More generally everyone who is a member and who suffers brings comfort to a wider group within that body. Our attitude to suffering and to comfort is often individualistic: Suffering refines and purifies the one who suffers. For Paul it purifies and sustains the body of Christ; it builds up the church.

Questions remain. We do not suffer because we are Christians; how then can we know anything of the comfort of which Paul writes? We can understand the help given by an encouraging word or a brave example, but how can we grasp the way comfort flows from one member of the body to another? That what Paul writes is true, we can observe when we read of those

who suffer in pioneer mission areas and in fascist and communist countries. Perhaps we shall only understand it in our own
lives when we take our faith more seriously, when we allow it
to disturb us more deeply. Then we will know a greater fellowship with others as we support them, share with them the comfort we receive from God, and participate in the comfort they
receive from him.

There is a final question. Many of those we try to comfort
are not Christians or are only half-hearted Christians; even the
suffering we meet in Christians has rarely anything to do with
their being Christians but is part of the general suffering of
humanity. What has this passage got to say to this? If we are
honest, we admit "Nothing"! Our passage deals with one particular theme, Christian suffering. We must not force it into saying
more than is in it. There is much elsewhere in Scripture that
relates to suffering in general. In our passage there is enough
to start us thinking—and comforting our fellow Christians without trying to find an answer to all suffering.

God Delivers (1:8–11)

The second theme in our passage concentrates on the
effect of Paul's suffering on himself and what he learned from
it. Paul writes about only one incident, but it was one in which
he came near to death. He does not tell us what it was, but the
Corinthians would have known of it, though they may not
previously have realized its gravity. Commentators have puzzled their heads as to what it was that happened to Paul: a
dangerous illness, mob violence, arrest and threat of execution,
shipwreck, capture by bandits? It could have been any of these.
In 11:23–29 he lists some of the trials he suffered and Acts tells
us of others. Whatever it was and wherever it happened ("Asia"
covers an area in which Paul was active for a long period), he
learned an important lesson from it.

The peril had been physical but the lesson spiritual. Paul
had been in danger of losing his life many times and had survived; this time there was no way in which he could imagine
himself escaping death. Yet in assessing the possibilities he had
left God out—and God had delivered him. We know as little
about the deliverance as we know about the danger. All we
know is that Paul saw it as the direct action of God. Where
neither human reason nor hope saw a solution God had created
one. We should note that, even though Paul speaks of God as

13

the one who raises the dead, he is not affirming here his belief that he will be raised after death. He has deliverance from earthly perils in mind. He would not be seeking, as he does in verse 11, the prayerful help of the Corinthians for his eternal salvation. He seeks it for the perils he still faces in his mission.

The prospect of death itself did not worry Paul. In Philippians 2:17 he says that he would have rejoiced "to be poured out as a libation" (i.e., to die) for his fellow Christians. Death would only have brought him to the closer presence of Christ (Phil. 1:19–26). But there are also places which suggest that there were times when he may not have eagerly looked forward to death. In 5:1–10 (see comment) Paul at one point seems to imply that to die would be to go out of existence for a period rather than to be fully united immediately to Christ. He might then justifiably fear death, not because of its pain but because it meant he might be, so to speak, out of commission for a period, the period until Christ's return and the general resurrection. His fear would not be of dying but of not being alive when Christ returned. If this is so we can see why he did not ask the Corinthians to pray that he should be made strong in the face of death and why he did ask them to continue to pray for his deliverance from death. Paul knew everyone must die sometime and was not worried by death as such.

Scholars have long recognized that Paul probably changed his mind in relation to what would happen to him at death before he came to write Philippians. He no longer feared a period after death when he would not be with Christ. For the present, however, believing that Christ was shortly to return and wishing to remain alive until then, he learned in his deliverance a new depth of trust in the God who had rescued him.

It is not that Paul reached the limits of human existence in the peril threatening him and thus learned to trust God and no longer to fear to die. Instead, faced with death and the possibility that God's purpose for him might not be fulfilled, his deliverance assured him that God had not abandoned the one he had chosen. Paul was still called to serve, and because of that he was secure. His confidence extends into the future: God will continue to deliver him from any perils in which he may find himself.

14   In his confidence Paul does not forget the Corinthians: They have their part to play and must help with their prayers. Their intercession has a place in the working out of God's plan.

But intercession should always lead forward to thanksgiving for its fulfillment. Paul has received a blessing from God—to live on to accomplish God's purpose. This blessing, his ministry to men and women, will bring rejoicing to many. Their thanksgiving will not therefore be disinterested. Thus in a different way than in verses 3–7 Paul's suffering brings good to others.

II Corinthians 1:12—2:4
Changes in Paul's Plans

The Corinthians have accused Paul of unnecessarily changing his travel plans. The heart of his answer lies in his affirmation that he is as steadfast as the gospel (1:15–22), but first he puts in a plea for understanding (1:12–14) and ends by explaining why he changed his travel arrangements (1:23—2:4).

A Plea for Understanding (1:12–14)

The transition from what precedes is not clear. Paul, as we all do in letters, may be simply beginning a fresh subject without feeling the need to connect it to what he has just written; or perhaps he feels they cannot pray for him unless they know he has been utterly sincere with them.

We all have had our words and actions misunderstood, especially when we have not expressed ourselves clearly. This was not the case with Paul, though it might have been (see II Peter 3:16). Paul has in fact been accused of being insincere in what he wrote. Though he might have admitted that he was sometimes hard to follow, he never would have allowed that he wrote intending to mislead. He penned no skillfully ambiguous sentences, used no subtle writer's tricks, and there is no need to read between the lines—all of which might be called "earthly wisdom." He wrote forthrightly and sincerely.

He looks back over his past conduct and believes he has no reason to have a bad conscience ("the testimony of our conscience") over the way he has behaved. His conduct is pure because it has been motivated and empowered by God. It is holy and sincere with a holiness and sincerity that come from God. He can boast because all is of God.

15

INTERPRETATION

The Corinthians have not totally misunderstood Paul, only partially, so he hopes they will come to full understanding. They have had more opportunity of doing this than other churches because of his lengthy stay with them and his many letters ("still more toward you"). When they do understand, he and they will have mutual pride in one another on the day of judgment (cf. I Thess. 2:19).

It is difficult to remain selfless if we have to defend ourselves against misunderstanding and reproach; any self-defense only brings us more firmly into the center of the picture. When Paul boasts in chapters 10—13, he is conscious of this peril (11:17). Here he escapes it by tracing his conduct back to God's grace. But when we do this it is easy to deceive ourselves, for many of those who have misled others in religion have been most sure they themselves were led by God. How then can we be sure of acting sincerely? It is not sufficient to say that our conscience will tell us. Our conscience is largely formed by the culture in which we live so that we may miss what God is saying to us, as do the Christian upholders of *apartheid* in South Africa. The conscience needs to be educated. When others criticize us we have then to take seriously what they say and re-examine the way we behave. We can have no cast-iron guarantee that we are right because our conscience does not accuse us.

Paul Vacillates No More Than God (1:15–22)

Paul has been reproached for changing his plans about visiting Corinth. It is not easy to determine what his original plans were or what led to their change. For discussions of scholarly opinion, see other commentaries. Much more interesting and important is the way in which he defends himself.

Similarly placed, most of us would begin by explaining the external factors which led us to change. Paul does not, though he comes to this later (1:23—2:4). His reasons at least were important, for he assures them that he wanted to come so that he could give them pleasure and be sent on by them to Jerusalem (vv. 15–16), presumably with the collection (chapters 8,9). Paul's main defense however does not lie in changed external factors. Summed up in two words, it is "trust God." That is where he ends though it is not where he begins. He asks the Corinthians two questions (v. 17), which probably repeat what has been said against him: that he had changed his plans for frivolous or unimportant reasons, that he calculated what he

16

would do on a "worldly" basis, for example, on grounds of expediency or to suit himself or to avoid trouble (the adjective "worldly" is formed from the favorite Pauline word "flesh"). Worldly people are those who are self-centered, deceive consciously, behave insincerely, or do not take God into account in what they plan. Paul has not been like that, saying one thing with his lips or pen and intending another in his heart ("ready to say Yes and No at once"). Paul of course does not deny that he has changed his mind; inflexibility can be as much the action of a worldly man as can fickleness. But if Paul has changed his mind it has been because he has been guided by the Spirit.

Paul has now lifted the discussion to a new plane: He is not a worldly man but one who depends on God. God is not double-tongued, so Paul is not double-tongued (v. 18). If accused of vacillation we might say, "Go and ask so-and-so; they'll tell you we are honest." We would call in witnesses who would testify to our straightforwardness. Paul calls in God but not for God to testify about Paul (God does not give special revelations like that) but to remind the Corinthians of the character of God. If Paul does not say "Yes and No" simultaneously, it is because God does not.

Paul makes the change from speaking of himself to speaking of God through the double meaning in the phrase "our word." It can refer both to his words about travel plans and to the gospel (the Word of God) which he preached and to which he goes on to refer in verse 19. The gospel cannot change its nature; no more can its preachers. Therefore Paul cannot be fickle. We would probably not dare to put our own reliability on a par with that of the gospel for we are very conscious of our own failures and we have too often met those whose lives have spoken a different gospel from the one they professed. Yet put another way we would agree with Paul. The character of those who preach the gospel or bear witness to it in their daily lives ought to be affected by that gospel. If we respond to the grace of God in Christ, then this should appear in the way we live, though not in reliability alone. God is not merely faithful but also loving and caring, and we should display the same in our lives. There is a logic in Paul's argument, but dare we use it? Are we too fearful of being unworthy of God?

The gospel is never "Yes" and "No" as if salvation lay in Christ today and in another tomorrow. It is always "Yes." How can this be so? Does not God often say "No" to our desires and

17

plans? Certainly, but with God there is no "Yes and No," leaving us in doubt. God's will is firm and fixed, however unclear it may appear to us, and God's salvation does not change from day to day. It is always the same in Christ. When, however, Paul says Jesus is God's "Yes" he has something much deeper in mind than the reliability of God's will: In Christ all the promises of God find their fulfillment (v. 20). In the first instance he was thinking of all the Old Testament prophesies which Christ fulfilled as son of David and expected Messiah. In him the justified live by faith (Hab. 2:4), and in him all nations are blessed in Abraham (Gen. 12:3; 18:18). All genuine human hopes and longings as expressed in the Old Testament are fulfilled in Christ. The New Testament often sets that fulfillment in terms of the chosen people and the law, for Christ is the true seed of Abraham (Gal. 3:16) and the end of the law (Rom. 10:4). There are also new hopes and longings in the New Testament. In the course of Christian history many of these have been worked out: slavery has disappeared; the sick, whether poor or wealthy, have been cared for. Legitimate hopes and longings also appear in society over and above those expressed in Scripture. These may be set in different terms in other cultures or religions. Some dream of a classless, raceless, or sexless society. If heaven will be such, ought not the church to be such now? Some desire to be at one with all creation in a profound unity and peace; they will discover that peace in Christ through whom all things were created and through whom all are reconciled to God. Insofar as these are legitimate hopes and longings, Christ is God's "Yes" to them. But he can also be God's "No" to every selfish and perverted longing of humanity, to every desire to "get rich quick," to dominate others, or to organize society for selfish advantage. Finally Christ is God's "Yes" to me. He gives me something on which I can found my life and build. If I mean something to him, then I must mean something to myself.

It is not only God who says "Yes" to us; we need to say "Yes" to him, to respond with our "Amen" (the word comes from Hebrew and means something like "faithfulness," "trustworthiness," and so "Yes"). It is as if Paul said, "Whenever you Corinthians respond in worship with your 'Amen' you affirm the trustworthiness of God, and so of me, for I have responded already with my whole life." It is impossible to say "Yes" to God and "No" to his apostle.

18

The position of Paul, Silvanus, and Timothy as the messengers of God confirms the validity of what they promise and the plans they make. Both they and the Corinthians (a tactful addition) are continually established in Christ. Since then they are all joined together in Christ, Paul cannot be fickle in his dealings with them. The name "Christ" and the word "commissioned" come from the same root. "Christ" means "anointed." Paul and his associates are then anointed, and in a Jewish context, this means they are given a special role to play in God's plans. They are also imprinted with God's seal. Seals are put on documents to authenticate them, and Paul with his fellow missionaries have been authenticated by God. Finally, God has put his Spirit into their hearts as a guarantee that they already possess the first installment of the fullness of God's salvation and are certain to receive it in its totality (v. 22*b*). Thus established, commissioned, sealed, and given the Spirit how can they be suspected of fickleness?

In this passage Paul has by-passed all the normal ways we use to settle misunderstandings. Suspected of vacillation by fellow Christians (that they were such is important), he quickly moves away from any kind of apology for his conduct into a deep consideration of the meaning of what God has done in Christ and of his own position in God's plans. Perhaps Paul fears that the Corinthians' doubts about himself may indicate doubts about his message. Any acceptance by the Corinthians of Paul and his plans must rest on an acceptance of his gospel and his place in God's salvation, a salvation which they know to be certain in Christ, the "Yes" of God. We are left with the question as to the level on which Christians should carry out a discussion of their intentions when there is misunderstanding. We cannot glibly assert "My intentions are God's intentions" lest our lives betray our assertion; nor can we surrender what we believe to be God's truth. And we must also remember that we and those with whom we disagree are together members of the body of Christ.

It does not look as if anyone prior to Paul had ever thought of calling Christ "God's Yes." In doing so he has brought out a new aspect of God's dealings with us in Christ in order to fit his situation and that of his readers. Here we see Christology being created (for another instance see 8:9). The way Paul understands Christ is not shaped by academic discussion but by the concrete situation. When we express Christ, do we do so in

19

purely academic terms or in terms of our situation and the situation of those we address?

Paul's Severity Derives from His Love (1:23—2:4)

After the magnificent "diversion" of 1:17–22, Paul now gives the kind of reasons any of us would give if accused of changing our plans needlessly, that is, a factual account of what led to this step. Paul does not regard this as unimportant, for he calls God to witness. This does not mean that he expects God to come down from heaven to refute him if he is wrong but rather that he puts his whole existence behind what he says: If he is wrong may his life be forfeit and he be rejected from salvation. It may sometimes be right to justify our conduct with theological arguments, but these must also be supported with an account of the facts. But even when Paul deals with these, the depth of his pastoral concern comes to the fore. "It reveals, more clearly perhaps than any passage in the New Testament, the essential qualification of the Christian minister—a heart pledged to his brethren in the love of Christ" (Denney, pp. 67–68).

Since the Corinthians know what has happened, Paul can be brief. He has had a difficult visit to Corinth (2:1; this is not the visit when he founded the church) and had then to write a difficult letter (2:3,9). Probably none of this has survived though some scholars think chapters 10—13 are part of it (see Introduction and "Opposition: Introduction"). Whatever we decide about that problem, however, will not further our understanding of the way Paul acts here as pastor.

Paul explains the basic reasons underlying his behavior. He could have simply scolded the Corinthians. Denouncing the sins of others brings a glow of self-satisfaction to the one who does it and to those who hear and are not the subjects of the denunciation. It rarely improves pastoral relations. Paul avoids this trap. He also goes out of his way to reject another easy but rarely effective method of exercising pastoral care: the claim to superior knowledge and therefore the right to order others about. "I am your father and know more about the world than you." "I have more experience of the world than you have." Paul as founder of the church would have had a good base from which to make that kind of claim. Instead he sets himself on their level, "we work with you" (1:24, "fellow workers"), and emphasizes cooperation in the gospel. Those in positions of pastoral care are given spiritual gifts for what they have to do, not so that they may feel important or act in a superior way to others. Paul knows the Christian faith of his converts (they stand firm in the faith; 1:24) and so he recognizes their independence. Anyone in a pastoral position has to learn to say "Yes" to the Christian experience of others as God has said "Yes" to his or her own. The relation between Paul and the Corinthians is not then just one of a friendly togetherness but belongs to the very nature of Christian existence which has set them both together in the body of Christ.

If Paul can accept their position and not attempt to dominate them, he still needs to explain why he did not visit them but instead wrote a letter. He did it to spare them another angry and painful scene (1:23; 2:2). Some disputes are best settled face to face. Paul decided this was not one of them. An encounter would not only have left them feeling bitter, but he himself would have suffered (2:3). When provoked he might not have held his tongue, and matters would only have been made worse.

So after much thought, "out of affliction and anguish of heart and with many tears" (2:4), he wrote a letter. We do not know what he actually wrote, but the present letter implies that it had the desired effect and that he and the Corinthians once again were seeing eye to eye. Joy and pain should be shared within the body of Christ. Earlier Paul had written of the mutual nature of affliction (1:3–11); joy can also be mutual (2:2–3). Were this not so Paul could not have written to them as he did and they would not have responded to his letter as they did.

Paul was dealing with those who were fellow members with him in the body of Christ. Many of those to whom we stand in a pastoral relation are not. Yet we cannot treat them differently. Since the basis of every pastoral relation is love, we have to love non-Christians in the same way as we love Christians. To both we give the same care, agonize over letters that need to be written, avoid angry encounters that get nowhere. Non-Christians may not, however, respond to us in the same way as Christians for we are not joined with them in the same fellowship. Yet even if our care is thrown back in our faces, we must still go on loving them in a pastoral relation.

When we think of a pastoral relation with others, whether in the church or not, another important difference with Paul appears. Paul acts individually; we almost always share our pastoral activity with others. The normal family has two parents,

21

and they need to act together. Even the parents of one-parent families share a pastoral relation toward their children with teachers and many others in the community. When, then, we exercise oversight we need to take into account what others are doing.

Today there is also a much wider corporate pastoral relation in which we are all involved because we live in a democracy. I may have an individual pastoral relation with a particular drug addict. I have also a corporate pastoral relation with all drug addicts through the attitude I adopt to legislation in respect to drugs and the provision of treatment clinics. In this way I can seek to help all addicts. This same corporate pastoral responsibility applies in many other areas of life for many of the relations which in Paul's day were possible only on a face to face basis but are now affected by legislative decisions. We may not be in jail to convert the jailer as Paul did in Philippi, but we have a responsibility to see that prisoners return to society as members fit to live in it. In our use or non-use of nuclear weapons we exercise a pastoral relationship, not only with people in our own nation and the one we fear but toward the whole world.

II Corinthians 2:5–11
Forgiveness

At some stage before Paul wrote the difficult letter of 2:3, there had been a troublesome incident in Corinth involving one particular member. This incident may have occurred during his painful visit (2:1) and be referred to also in 7:5–13, or it may have been subsequent to that visit. It is unlikely that he is referring, as some have suggested, to the man who had committed incest (I Cor. 5:1). Paul does not name the offender nor tell us either his offense or the penalty imposed. The Corinthians would have known all this. It was probably not a personal offense against Paul (v. 5; cf. v. 10), though the person may have attacked Paul indirectly by attacking his teaching. To speak of the offender as "punished" (RSV; v. 6) is too strong a term. The Greek word need mean no more than a rebuke or censure. We should certainly not think of the offender as excommunicated (see further on 10:1–6 and 13:1–10 for the use of discipline in the early church). He may have been prayed for publicly or rebuked by the leaders of the church.

The penalty had been imposed by the community. While our translation (RSV) speaks of this action as one taken by "the majority" (v. 6), it would be wrong to think of a decision taken after a formal vote or of a majority/minority division within the community. All the word signifies is that there was no serious opposition to the decision. The penalty achieved its purpose. This was probably due less to its actual severity than to the common conscience of the community bearing in on the offender. Official decisions unsupported by the majority in a community rarely work. Still less will they bring an offender to that repentance which is their primary purpose. Sometimes though that purpose is taken as the safeguarding of the purity of the community. When this takes precedence the end result is often pride and hypocrisy. Where repentance is sought in loving concern, both community and offender grow in faith and grace.

The offender's penitence has now moved Paul to write. It is time to suspend the penalty, for the punishment has been enough (v. 6). In advising the church to forgive, Paul suggests two reasons why they should do so: (i) to save the offender from plunging too deeply into grief and self-condemnation, and so perhaps to forsake the church and return to paganism or to commit suicide; (ii) if the community does not forgive, it may be overcome by Satan (v. 11), though Paul does not envisage this happening at this stage. Now is the time for the community to take a new step in love and to forgive (v. 8). We note that Paul is more concerned about Satan's gaining control of the community than of the offender. The community that is unwilling to forgive will not merely impair its own effectiveness as a genuine community in Christ but may even destroy itself.

It is never easy to forgive. So Paul pledges his own forgiveness for the offender since it was at his instruction in the severe letter that the penalty was originally imposed (v. 9). He wants to be at one with the church in forgiveness, offering it as "in the presence of Christ." The basis for our forgiving others is the forgiveness we have already received through Christ (Col. 3: 13). It is only because we have been restored that we can restore others, and if we do not forgive we cannot expect forgiveness (Matt. 6:14–15).

23

There is an odd ambivalence at times in Paul's attitude to his churches. He does not lord it over their faith (1:24); he begs them to act in a Christian way (v. 8); yet he also requires their obedience (v. 9). This ambivalence may arise in part out of his passionate nature, as he rings the changes between pleading and demanding, and in part out of his position. He is the representative of Christ and speaks and acts for him; he can therefore demand obedience to himself as Christ's representative. As we exercise our pastoral care, we often face the same dilemma, and it is all too easy to concentrate on demanding rather than on pleading.

II Corinthians 2:12–13
Paul's Anxiety

In all Christian work tension appears when we have to balance one necessary activity against another. In Paul's case it came both from the need to go to new areas to evangelize and to minister to the churches he had already established. He had gone to Troas and his preaching was more than acceptable—a door was being opened. He had also sent Titus to Corinth, and he was gasping for news of what was happening. Had Titus been repulsed and was all his work there in danger? So Paul left Troas and started off to meet Titus somewhere en route (he could check for him in each church on the way: Philippi, Thessalonica, Beroea, Athens). At this point the story breaks off without letting us know what happened. If it is this story, as it probably is, which is continued at 7:5, then we learn there that when Paul met up with Titus he received good news and his anxiety about the Corinthians was resolved. It is because of the strange break in the story at this point that some scholars take 2:14—7:4 to be from another part of Paul's correspondence with the Corinthians (see Introduction and notes on 2:14–17 and 7:5–16).

PART TWO

Paul's Present Ministry to the Corinthians

II CORINTHIANS 2:14—7:4

II Corinthians 2:14–17
The Aroma of Christ

With 2:14–17 there is a sharp change both in the subject matter and in the tone of the letter, which for the first time becomes polemical. Paul breaks off the discussion of his movements and his desire for news of Corinth to enter on a fresh line of self-defense. The radical nature of the break has led many scholars to assume that 2:14 begins a portion of another letter which a later editor has attached to 1:1—2:13 (see Introduction). If a fresh letter begins here, we have no idea what preceded it or why Paul should be thankful. If 2:14–17 continues the same letter as 1:1—2:13, we still are not clear why Paul should be thankful since he does not yet mention the good news Titus brought from Corinth. Perhaps he assumes the Corinthians know it, and he can therefore go ahead and rejoice without telling them why. Whatever we decide about the integrity of our letter, 2:14—7:4 is not an unimportant parenthesis.

In opening his self-defense (v. 17) Paul uses three pictures. The first is often taken to suggest Christ as a victorious Roman general riding into Rome with his conquered trophies and victims (including Paul) led along behind him (v. 14a). But Paul regarded himself as a soldier of Christ rather than as his prisoner of war. The image then is difficult, as anyone who consults the commentaries and translations will see. We probably come nearer the true idea when we realize that the Greek word

25

rendered "leads us in triumph" often is used without any idea of triumph, as meaning "display publicly, make known." With this meaning the first picture joins up neatly with the second. "Thanks be to God who displays us publicly in Christ and makes known the fragrance of the knowledge of Christ (or "himself"; there is little difference in essential meaning) through us everywhere." Paul is God's chosen and public means of spreading the gospel and the gospel has an attractiveness all of its own. Because of this Paul can be thankful. (The reference to fragrance would have meant much more in the first century world with its open drains and foul smells than it does to us.) God uses his servants not just to expose human sin but to spread abroad the beauty of the gospel. Unfortunately many Christians are more enthusiastic in denouncing evil than in proclaiming the beauty of Christ and the gospel.

The third picture, "aroma," carries on the second, but the beauty lies now in the preacher rather than in what he preaches, and it is God who is aware of the aroma. The image comes from the Old Testament idea of the sweet smell or "pleasing odor" of sacrifices offered to God (e.g., Gen. 8:21; Exod. 29:18; Lev. 1:9; cf. Eph. 5:2; Phil. 4:18). The activity of those who make known the gospel, whether in formal preaching or daily life, is like a sacrifice offered to God. So the worship and consecrated lives of believers are often described as sacrificial offerings (Rom. 12:1; Phil. 4:18; Heb. 13:15–16; I Peter 2:5). These can be presented to God only in and through the sacrifice of Christ. Paul's claim, or anyone's, to be the aroma of Christ might seem arrogant had not Paul immediately added "Who is sufficient for these things?" Whatever we do in Christian service, we do only because God has made us into the kind of people we are (cf. 3:5–6).

A change of direction leads us to think of the effect of the gospel on those who hear it: Mediated through Paul, and through us, it divides humanity into two groups, those who are being saved and those who are perishing. Paul uses present tenses here because he is describing a processs which may yet be reversed. Those who are now perishing may be saved and those who are now being saved may perish. To one group the fragrance is a most deadly smell ("from death to death") bringing death but to the other group a life-giving odor bringing life.

26

Now Paul is ready to defend himself from those who have attacked him. This self-defense continues through most of the remainder of the letter. There were many in the ancient world who charged fees for their teaching about the ultimate things of life. Since they lived by their fees they had to please their hearers. Paul may well have regarded those troubling the church as such—and they may have thought the same about him. He avers therefore that he has never hawked around God's word only to those who could pay, as others ("like so many") may have done. Paul regularly refused payment from the churches to which he preached (see on 11:7–10 and 12:14–18). He was then under no pressure to adjust his message to please his hearers. He was no electronic evangelist continually appealing for money. There is nothing more effective for the spread of the gospel than the sincerity of those who know and love it, and any genuine sincerity starts and ends with the knowledge that we live before God and act for him. We are then the aroma of Christ to the world. This is a tremendous responsibility, and who is "sufficient" for it? Paul goes on to answer this in the next section.

II Corinthians 3:1–18
A Minister of the New Covenant

In this chapter Paul contrasts his ministry with that of Moses and the new covenant in Christ with the old covenant mediated by Moses. He probably does this because those who have been troubling the Corinthians have overstressed the Old Testament and understressed the newness of Christ. In verses 1–6 he lays the foundation for his argument by introducing a set of contrasts between the old way with Moses and the new way with Christ and then develops this in the remainder of the chapter.

Life Comes from the Spirit (3:1–6)

Paul begins with a continuation of his defense of his ministry. As today so in the ancient world, when people go traveling they often take with them letters written by friends commending them to friends of their friends. Paul himself sometimes commends his friends to others (cf. Rom. 16:1–2; II Cor. 8:

27

22-24). Those who were disturbing the Corinthian church had come to it hoping to be accepted on the basis of such letters—we do not know the identity of those who wrote commending them. Paul sees no need of any such letters for himself; his sincerity is enough to commend him. If however the Corinthians really want such letters, then Paul can offer many—the Corinthian Christians themselves. Unlike the letters brought by his opponents, his are not written with ink on paper but by the Holy Spirit on human hearts. Paul can point happily to these letters for he knows the depth of the love of God in the lives of the Corinthians. He knows this because he is not the writer but only the deliverer of these letters; their true writer is Christ.

It might seem that Paul had now made his point. Those who were troubling the church could never produce as many letters or letters as good. Yet what Paul has said so far is only a launching pad for what he wants to go on to say about the new convenant. So instead of contrasting the lives of the Corinthians to letters written with ink on paper, he contrasts them with letters chiseled on stone, for he has in mind the original stone tablets of the Ten Commandments (Exod. 31:18; Deut. 9:10). This contrast had already appeared in the Old Testament when Jeremiah prophesied that the new covenant would be written on hearts rather than on stone (31:33). Ezekiel had spoken of the change from hearts of stone to hearts of flesh (11:19; 36:26; note that "human hearts" in II Cor. 3:3 is literally "hearts of flesh"). Paul then packs into the last words of verse 3 a lot of thought, which he draws out later in the chapter. The immediate implication of what he says is that he himself belongs to the new covenant while those he writes against cling too closely to the old.

Before Paul can go on to this main argument he has another point to clear up. At the end of 2:16 he raised the question "Who is sufficient for these things?" (The words rendered "competence," "competent" in 3:5,6 in the second edition of the RSV are the same as that rendered "sufficient.") Paul now answers his own question "I am." He can affirm this because the Spirit has been at work in the hearts of the Corinthians who are his commendatory letters. Those, then, who wish may read the Corinthians and see his competence. But Paul is not asserting a confidence in his own ability. He is well aware of his own weakness; he also knows the saving power of Christ. His confidence is therefore before and toward God. He needs neither the recognition of human beings nor their opinions to bolster him up, for all is through Christ. Both Paul's success and his competency come from God.

Having got that point out of the way, Paul returns to his main argument and picks up and extends the language and ideas which had begun to appear in verse 3. There he had introduced the contrast between the covenant made at the time of Moses and another later covenant. This later covenant is now called a "new covenant," a term deriving from Jeremiah 31:31–34. Paul's readers already know the term, for in the form he taught them to observe the Eucharist were the words "This . . . is the new covenant in my blood" (I Cor. 11:25).

Since the term comes from the Old Testament, Paul's contrast is not a simple one between Judaism and Christianity or between the Old Testament as law and the New as gospel. Neither the old covenant nor the new began when people approached God and offered him their piety and obedience and asked him in return to give them salvation. In both covenants it is God who makes the approach and offers salvation. The difference between them, which Paul draws out, lies in the point that one is written and the other is of the Spirit. It would however be wrong to apply this distinction as if it were the distinction between written words and their meaning or between man-made laws and divine spiritual laws (both covenants were given by God). It would also be wrong to apply it to justify the drawing out from a passage of some spiritual or allegorical meaning not found in the ordinary or literal sense of the words. Finally if the written code is the Jewish Law, when Paul speaks of the Spirit he is not thinking, as some have sought to maintain, of the spirit of the law as expressed in the two great commandments (Mark 12:29–31).

It is true that Paul expresses himself in apparently different ways about the Jewish Law. Since it comes from God, it is good and holy (Rom. 7:12,14), but now as he looks back on the time before he became a Christian he sees it as a written code which separated him from God and brought him death (cf. Rom. 8:2,5; 7:10). A written code which we are supposed to keep brings the danger that our attention is taken up with our success and failure in keeping it, though of course this danger can also appear without a written code. What is generally accepted in society as good or bad and what our conscience approves or disapproves function in the same way. Such things are seen as

29

standards against which to measure ourselves. Behind such "measuring" lies a selfish desire to rule our own lives and assert our independence of God by winning our own salvation. If so, we die, for the "written code kills." If we are to live, life must come not from some code of behavior but from God; thus it is the Spirit that "gives life."

In the following verses Paul continues to contrast the two covenants against those either in the church or those influencing it from outside who were overstressing aspects of the old covenant.

The Ministries of the Old and New Covenants (3:7–18)

Paul now appears temporarily to drop his personal defense for a complex discussion of an important Old Testament passage (Exod. 34:29–35; this recounts the giving of the Ten Commandments to Moses). Yet Paul's personal situation and what he now writes are probably related because those whom he was opposing were using arguments from the Old Testament to sustain their position. As we have seen, Paul was preparing in 3:1–6 for what he is now going to say (note the words and ideas in vv. 3,6 which reappear in our section; "minister" and "dispensation" are from the same Greek root). He is therefore not now drawn off into a side issue. His final words in verse 6 claimed that his ministry and that of his associates was a ministry of the new covenant. The old covenant had its glory, but it was one that faded (v.7; "splendor" and "glory" are the same word in Greek). The new covenant possesses a glory that grows (v. 18). Paul and his associates as ministers of the new covenant grow with that growing glory. Thus when Paul returns in chapter 4 to his own personal situation, he is in a position to make new claims for his ministry.

The present section interprets Exodus 34:29–35 from a Christian perspective. What Paul writes is not easy to follow, for he uses a type of argument to which we are not accustomed (see "Paul and the Old Testament"). Moreover in his interpretation, Paul probably uses Jewish tradition, which had developed after the Old Testament was written but with which he had become familiar during his rabbinic training. (Details can be found in the more academic commentaries.) What Moses received was a written law, or more accurately, a law carved in letters on stone (v. 7; cf. v. 3). This written law was a code (i) of death (v. 7; cf. v. 6 "the written code kills"), (ii) of condemnation (v. 9),

30

and (iii) it was a code which had lost its splendor (vv. 10–11). By contrast Paul's new covenant ministry is of the Spirit, with greater and more permanent splendor, and it ministers righteousness to all humanity. All who live under the new covenant enjoy these blessings.

The law came from God and had then a splendor of its own (cf. Rom. 7:12,14), but given the greater splendor that comes with Christ, the law only brings death and condemnation. Paul the Jew believed the law gave life (cf. Ps. 119); Paul the Christian knows its result is death (cf. Rom. 8:2; Gal. 3:10–14,21,23), and with death comes condemnation, for the law makes plain where we have failed and gives us no hope.

Here Paul introduces an idea about the law which we do not find in the Old Testament: the fading of its glory. This does not mean that the law had been slowly losing importance and influence from the time of its inauguration. Rather, the law lacks permanent validity, a point which is seen with the coming of Christ. In its day the law had sufficient glory to dazzle the eyes of the Israelites; in Christ there is an even brighter light. The bright light we find it hard to stare at fades steadily into nothingness when the sun shines behind it. So the ministry of the Spirit which comes through Christian ministers like Paul brings a greater splendor, greater than any splendor any minister of the old covenant, even Moses its greatest minister, could provide. We do not have to wait for the end of all things for this ministry of the Spirit; it exists now (cf. v. 18), and it not only frees from condemnation but gives righteousness. It brings us into a new relation with the God who saves. Here Paul touches on the great themes he developed in Galatians and Romans. The Corinthians will of course know these themes from his original mission among them.

As a Jew Paul had no way of approaching God other than through the law, and he believed it brought him life. As a Christian he sees it all from a new angle. When we become Christians, or come to realize the importance of our Christian faith, we look back at what we were and obtain a new perspective on it. We may not have come to Christ or to a clear understanding of his importance from the law; perhaps we came from another religion or we previously believed that good behavior is the way to please God. While these convictions may have seemed earlier to have great value, now they appear poor in comparison with the splendor of Christ.

31

INTERPRETATION

The second section (vv. 12–18) is one of the most difficult in Second Corinthians. This is partly caused by uncertainties as to its translation. We shall accept that of the Revised Standard Version; it is as likely to be correct as any other. The difficulties are usually well explained though not solved in the more academic commentaries. Paul's text is still Exodus 34:29–35. He now pays particular attention to the veil on the face of Moses. According to Exodus, Moses always wore the veil except when he was speaking with God in the tent of meeting or had just come out from it to pass on to the Israelites what God had said to him. He wore the veil apparently for the sake of the Israelites, since when his face shone with the glory (splendor) of God they were afraid to come near him. Paul explains the veil in a different way: Moses wore it lest the people should see how after he had come from speaking with God the glory gradually faded from his face.

As Paul goes on he takes a further and even stranger step with regard to the veil. He moves it from the face of Moses to the minds of the Israelites by way of the idea of a veil on the Old Testament itself. If Paul's reasoning in these changes leaves us a little cold at times, we can at least see what he means by them and agree with the conclusions he reaches. The fading splendor on Moses' face represents the passing of the old covenant (i.e., the law of Moses). The veil on the minds of the Jews represents (i) their failure to read the Old Testament correctly, that is, to find Christ in it, and, more importantly, (ii) the failure of the Jews of Paul's own time to accept Christ when he was preached to them (note the repeated "to this day," vv. 14–15). Romans 9—11 show us that Paul was greatly worried by this failure. There he looks forward to the time when the fullness of the Gentiles will come to Christ and the fullness of the Jews will follow. Of course he knows that some Jews had indeed already become Christians; he himself had. When this happens it is as if a veil were removed so that they see their promised Messiah. It was removed from his own mind at his conversion. He fears however it has not been fully removed from all Jewish-Christians, in particular from those who oppose him in Corinth, for they still keep the law too much in the center of their teaching.

Jews who failed to accept Christ did so because their minds were dulled ("hardened," v. 14). In Romans 11:7–8 (cf. 11:25) Paul ascribes this hardening to God. Since he uses similar language here he probably intends the same in both places: God

32

has dulled the minds of the Jews. He is responsible for the veil on their minds as he once was for its presence on the face of Moses, for Moses can be assumed to have been obeying God when he put the veil on his face. Yet even if God is responsible for the veil on the hearts of Jews, that does not free them from blame if they reject Christ. When Paul dealt with this problem in Romans, he argued that Israel was still morally responsible for its failure (9:30—10:21). Paul cannot excuse those of his own race, and yet he cannot really see why with the Old Testament in their hands they fail to recognize Christ. It has all been blindingly clear to him since his conversion. So he speaks of hardened minds. We are often puzzled by those who are brought up within the Christian community and then fail to continue in active Christian life. We may feel inclined like Paul to say "their minds were hardened." We need to go on then also to say as he did that such people are themselves responsible. It is only when we recognize this that we shall move to end their situation. How will they hear if no one brings them the gospel (Rom. 10:14)!

It might appear that Paul was setting out to describe the relation of the Old and New Testaments or the people of God before and after Christ, but he rarely deals with intellectual problems such as these. It is a pastoral problem in dealing with the Corinthians that has led him into this discussion. Their only holy book was the Old Testament, and they probably depended too much on it and its laws. Paul wishes them to pay less attention to the Law and more to Christ. Probably also there were those either in the community or infiltrating it from outside who were criticizing Paul and his methods and using the Old Testament as the basis of their criticism. Paul then refutes them with an argument drawn from that very same Old Testament.

Whatever it was that sparked off this discussion it resulted in Paul being turned aside from the direct defense of his ministry. What he has just been saying applies to all Christians. In fact when he began in verse 12 with "*we* have such a hope" and not with "we have such a ministry," he was beginning to lose sight of the attacks on his own ministry. All Christians have a hope which frees them from the fear of death and condemnation and which enables them to share in the splendor that is permanent (vv. 7–11). Hope gives boldness (v. 12) and as Moses was bold enough to meet God within the tent of meeting with unveiled face so "we all" see the glory of the Lord without veiled faces.

33

Yet though Moses veiled his face when he came out of the tent, we should not attempt to veil the glory of God which is in our lives. We should be bold to confess Christ by allowing his glory to be seen in us.

Verse 17 contains one of the most debated sentences in Scripture, "Now the Lord is the Spirit." When considering this, it is wrong to try to confine Paul within the limits of a doctrine of the Trinity that was developed after his time. In verse 17 Paul is carrying further the argument of verse 16. That verse depends on Exodus 34:34 where "the Lord" means God. The New Testament regularly applies to Christ texts from the Old Testament which so use "Lord." Thus for Paul "the Lord" in verse 16 is Christ. In verse 17 the first "Lord" is also Christ. The second could have the same reference, but it is better to refer it to God because "the Spirit of the Lord" is a frequent phrase in both Testaments for the Holy Spirit, that is, "the Spirit of God." In verse 6 Paul had introduced the Spirit as life-giving. When people become Christians (v. 16), they turn to the Lord, that is, Christ, who in fact has this same life-giving power ("the Lord is the Spirit"). Life means freedom, and so where the Spirit is there is freedom. Christians who are free are free from the Law of the old covenant, and their justification comes from Christ and not from doing the Law. Though Paul equates the activity of Christ and of the Spirit in the lives of Christians, he does not actually identify them (he distinguishes them in 13:14).

Those who turn to the Lord have then a new hope, a new freedom and a new boldness. Above all they are changed and this change comes from the Lord who is the Spirit. There follows another of those triumphant sentences which break out from Paul from time to time (v. 18). We can forgive him the obscure argument, which has preceded, for the present glorious affirmation. God is not hidden from us by any veil on our faces or hearts; we see his unutterable glory. We see it in Christ when he is preached to us, when we read of him in Scripture, when we meet him in the Eucharist. We see it also in our fellow Christians, in their love to us and to all men and women. When we see that glory, when we see Christ, we ourselves are changed. Every day we are changed by the people we meet. For good or ill they leave their imprint on us, and the stronger their personality, as it were, the greater their impact. How much greater then the impact of the risen Christ! If husbands and wives grow more like one another as the years go by, how much more shall we as we live with Christ and his people be changed into his likeness. But just as we cannot save ourselves, so we cannot change ourselves into his likeness. Only the power of the risen Christ can accomplish genuine and lasting change in us. Moses and the Law had not the power to do that for the Jews. Through Christ we are changed from one degree of glory to another, until at last we are entirely transformed into his likeness and glory. This transformation is one of Paul's constant themes (Rom. 12:2; 8:29; I Cor. 15:49–51; Phil. 3:21).

Paul and the Old Testament

Paul's argument throughout 3:7–18 has been based on Old Testament Scripture. For him that Scripture had been given by God and, therefore, was basic. Though its splendor may yet fade, Paul draws from it the clues that help him to understand what is happening to him. From Jeremiah (31:31–34) came the idea of a new covenant, which Paul now sees fulfilled. While this appears straightforward, some of the other ways in which he argues from the Old Testament are difficult, not merely to understand but to follow through. The Old Testament does not tell us that the splendor faded gradually from the face of Moses, for it used the veil on the face of Moses in a different manner from Paul. Paul has probably here used Jewish tradition deriving from a period later than the Old Testament. Even granted that, there is a greater difficulty: How can such an insignificant event as the veiling of his face by Moses be interpreted to produce important conclusions about Christ? Basically Paul argues here the way he does because he believes the Old Testament was written for our (Christians') benefit (Rom. 15:4; I Cor. 9:10). Often he uses it in the way any writer might quote from an authoritative book to support what he is saying. But there are times when, as here (cf. Gal. 4:21–31), his mode of argument is foreign to the way we argue. He is in fact following contemporary exegetical practices as used in the Jewish and Greek worlds. He does not deduce the results logically from the text in the way we would. We have however to bear in mind that it was not primarily his reading of Exodus that convinced Paul about the deficiencies of the law and its fading splendor. It was the experience of his conversion. This was like the lifting of a veil from his eyes, and so he uses Exodus 34:29–35 to explain his experience. We would not use the Old Testament in the way

35

Paul does here, for all biblical scholars now stress the need to use the simple or plain meaning of the words of Scripture. They no longer find valid, ways of reading the text that seem to draw from it, by playing with words, a meaning that the original author never thought of.

There are other examples of this use of the Old Testament in 6:14; 8:15; 9:6. In each case Paul moves from what is true in the natural world to a spiritual truth. It seems to us he already knows the spiritual truth he wishes to emphasize and apparently just looks for an Old Testament text which he can transform into the meaning he wants. If we have doubts about his method of arguing, that is not however to say his conclusions are wrong.

It may even seem odd to us that Paul founds so much of what he says on the Old Testament for we tend to start with the New. We do not accept all that is in the Old: We eat pork; we do not offer blood sacrifices; we do not think the world was made in six days. Paul however had no New Testament. The one book he had in common with his supporters and his opponents was the Old Testament. He therefore had to use it. If occasionally Paul uses it in a way strange to us, this should not lead us to belittle it. Jews who do not have the New Testament still hear God speak to them in the Old and have been sustained by it through many persecutions.

II Corinthians 4:1–15
Treasure in an Earthen Vessel

Paul's Faithfulness to the Gospel (4:1–6)

Paul returns now to the direct defense of his ministry as we see from the appearance of the word itself (4:1; cf. 3:6–11 where "dispensation" translates the same Greek root). Probably because some people had been overstressing the Old Testament he had argued in chapter 3 that his ministry was superior to that of Moses. Now he defends himself against more general accusations. The verses may be grouped in sets of two (vv. 1–2, 3–4, 5–6), with each of the first two couplets rising to a kind of minor climax and the third to a triumphant major climax, "the light of the knowledge of the glory of God in the face of Christ."

Paul begins the first pair of verses with something very basic to his own ministry: He did not obtain that ministry by his own efforts or study (M.Div. with commendation!) but through God's mercy. He was always conscious that he had once persecuted the church and that it had taken God's action to change him to be God's apostle (I Cor. 15:9–10; Gal. 1:13–16). As the recipient of God's mercy, he could not be other than faithful to God's mission and be ready to carry on without losing heart. God does not forsake those whom he has called to any type of pastoral responsibility; they exercise their responsibility through his mercy; even parents do so, for it is by his mercy that they have their children. To remember God's mercy then will sustain us when things seem to go wrong.

Nothing disheartens us more than the accusations of those we set out to help. Accusations had been made against Paul. He does not list them, but we can infer that he was charged with acting deceptively and secretly and with "adjusting" God's word (cf. 2:17) to suit his own convenience (v. 2). Perhaps he was accused of tampering with the Word of God because he broke away from some of the many laws of the Old Testament. Preachers have often been tempted to adjust their preaching to satisfy some group in their congregation. The "word" has been watered down ("tamper" was used of those who adulterated food and wine). The truths of biblical criticism have been withheld so as not to disturb the elderly or some outspoken group. The need for repentance from actual and precise sins has not been preached, or only a narrow spectrum of sins (e.g., those connected with sex) has been attacked so as not to annoy the lukewarm, the evangelistic, or those without a social conscience. The call to firm committal and decision has been avoided so as not to drive away good contributors. Preachers apart, many people trying to achieve some apparently good end have been tempted to maneuver and manipulate others without those others being aware of it, and all for the sake of the supposed good purpose.

In the second pair of verses (3–4), Paul seems to answer some who have picked on the failure of his gospel to win everyone and, therefore, criticized him. If, however, eyes have been veiled to the light of the gospel (Paul picks up here the idea he used in Chapter 3), it has only been the eyes of those who have been perishing. The fault does not lie in his preaching but in Satan ("the god of this world") who has prevented them from understanding what he says. If this seems an easy way of explaining unbelief, let us recall the pressures under which Paul and all the early church worked. They preached in the market place; some believed, others did not. To the preachers who had found wonderful joy and freedom in Christ it seemed unbelievable, at least in human terms, that their hearers should not all see the truth as clearly as themselves. The only possible solution was a supernatural one. A similar kind of solution had been offered in 3:14, only there God was held to have been responsible. Scripture uses both types of explanation (cf. II Sam. 24:1 where God incites David to number the people, but Satan does so in I Chron. 21:1).

Is such a supernatural understanding of unbelief satisfactory? Unbelief is solid fact and requires some kind of explanation. But explanations are not easy. One moment we blame the devil, the next materialism, communism, liberalism, or the spirit of the age. If we cling to the supernatural solution, we run the danger of not entering into the minds of those who reject the gospel. Simplistic solutions which trace the cause of unbelief to Satan are attractive. They cannot be said to be wrong, for there is always something irrational about evil. Unbelief does not necessarily yield to reason and understanding. When however we stress the supernatural aspect there is the danger that we allow the appeal to Satan to cut the nerve of any effort to evangelize sympathetically. Such an appeal may lift from us the need to enter with compassion into the lives of those who reject Christ. It is easy to use Satan as an excuse for the unbelief of others when the fault may lie in our own failure in the presentation of the gospel—and it is not only preachers who present it. We can never then resign ourselves into accepting the unbelief of others by attributing it to Satan and using that as an excuse for doing nothing. We must always continue lovingly to understand those to whom we present the gospel and to seek to explain and interpret it in our words and living so that they will give it a willing hearing.

In the final pair of verses (5–6), Paul attempts to refute the accusation that in his preaching he has been too much concerned with himself. It is easy to see how some people could have picked up this idea. The Corinthians have forced him to talk about himself. He has advised his converts to imitate him (I Cor. 4:16; 11:1). When people proclaim the gospel, what they proclaim can never be dissociated from their words and actions.

The gospel is not a set of abstract truths to be announced but a way of life to be lived. Admit this involvement and the danger cannot be avoided that there will be times when the believer will get in the way of the message. If the gospel is mediated by people, though its truth does not depend on the purity of their lives, its immediate appeal will.

In rejecting these accusations Paul again affirms the essence of his gospel: Jesus Christ is Lord (v. 5). Jesus, who once lived in Palestine, was crucified, and rose from the grave, has Paul's allegiance. He gives it neither to pagan god nor emperor ("lord" was commonly applied to both) nor even to the Jewish God (who is also called "Lord") except insofar as he is known through Jesus Christ, his likeness (v. 4). Since Christ is the Lord of his life, we might have expected Paul to go on and say that he was Christ's slave (this is a more accurate rendering than "servant") and that he therefore obeyed his Lord in serving the Corinthians. Paul cuts out the middle stage of the argument and moves directly to himself as their slave. It is relatively easy to say "I am God's slave," but something in us rebels when we have to say "I am their slave." We are as good as the next man or woman. But the Christian community is not one in which members are always aware of their rights and think themselves as good as the next. It functions only when each behaves as slave to all the others (cf. Mark 10:42–44). If the Corinthians could only grasp Paul's sincerity when he says he is their slave, then all the accusations against him would be seen in their true light and disappear.

All this might sound negative and overdefensive. Paul does not wish to leave it like that so he affirms the light that comes from God through Christ. Note the piling up of words, "the light of the gospel of the glory of Christ, who is the likeness of God" (v. 4), "the light of the knowledge of the glory of God in the face of Christ" (v. 6). The words pour out because Paul is overwhelmed with the greatness of God in Christ. It is all about light and seeing, a wonderful answer to accusations of underhandedness and veiling. It was on the road to Damascus that the light first shone into his heart. That outward light was a symbol of the glory of Christ streaming into his heart. Just as God once chased away darkness by commanding the light to shine at creation (Gen. 1:3), so he shone in Paul's heart to give the light of the new creation (II Cor. 5:17). The gospel is light and brings light and knowledge to the souls of those who open up to it. The

39

light is the brightness or glory (i.e., splendor) with which Christ and God shine. We cannot separate Christ and God. The brightness of God is seen in the face of Christ; Christ is the likeness of God. And the glory of God, which we expect to see in the ascended and exalted Christ, cannot be separated from that same glory revealed in the cross.

Life Through Death (4:7–15)

Paul finished his last paragraph on a high note: God had shone in his heart and had given him an important ministry. But his life would not have looked important to an independent observer. To all appearances he was no more than an earthenware vessel, a cheap clay pot. Precious objects and treasures were, however, regularly kept in such pots. What treasure then is contained in the clay pot that is Paul? The answer is certainly not an immortal soul or divine spark kept in a perishable and mortal body. The clue comes from the preceding paragraph (*this* treasure). It may be either Paul's ministry or the light which shone in his heart when he became a Christian or the knowledge of the glory of God in the face of Christ. In fact these three cannot be clearly marked off from one another. The light which shone in Paul's heart on the Damascus road made him a Christian, gave him his ministry, and brought him to see the glory of God in the face of Christ. What he says here of himself is true of every Christian and is seen most clearly when daily life is given up to the ministry of others—and all daily life should be a ministry to others.

For Paul a correlative of the recognition of human weakness is always the opportunity it gives to God. So the success of his ministry and the vitality of his Christian existence (neither should be measured in human terms) do not spring from his own ability and dedication but from the transcendent power of God. Paul draws out what this means with four vivid contrasts (vv. 8,9). By all human reckoning he ought to be crushed, driven to despair, feel himself forsaken and destroyed because of what he has been through. It is useless to speculate what past incidents in his life Paul has in mind. He lists some of his trials in 11:23–28, but here he does not seem to be thinking primarily of physical suffering. Far worse is the anguish of mind that comes when we see those we love get into trouble, and Paul has seen this happen to the Corinthians. Despite his care, they are failing to follow through in their Christian living. We might use

40

other terms to describe the anxieties that come to us, not from the general human situation but because we try to live as Christians. We do good and our goodness is ascribed to an attempt to curry popularity. We are profoundly perplexed when we try to apply Christianity to the terrifying problems of modern society: Is unemployment worse than inflation? Does the possession of nuclear weapons endanger or preserve society? We are frustrated in our attempts to carry out some reform in an organization or community of which we are members.

The pressures on Paul to which he refers did not get him down. God's transcendent power enabled him to endure. Some people stubbornly refuse to give in to adversity; with stiff upper lip they endure whatever fate throws at them. We admire them. But that was not how Paul endured, for the source of his strength lay not within himself but in the grace of God. God's power was made perfect in his weakness (12:9). That power is also always there with us to balance every outside circumstance and every interior thought that would bring us down. The promise is not that our troubles will pass away with time or that they only appear to be troubles or that a way out of them will eventually be found. The troubles are real and may never disappear, yet the power of God is there to bring us through them.

Paul generalizes the four contrasts of verses 8–9 into three more in verses 10–12. Of these the first two are parallel, but the third breaks new ground. The affliction, perplexity, et cetera, of verses 8–9 are rephrased as "carrying in the body the death of Jesus" and "being given up to death for Jesus' sake." Paul's thought progresses naturally here for the treasure of Jesus was also in a cheap earthenware vessel—his human existence. There he had been afflicted in every way, perplexed, persecuted, struck down. At first sight we might hesitate to apply "perplexed" to Jesus. Did he not always know what to do? But was he not perplexed when he thought of the hungry and poor? Should he turn stones into bread? This and other temptations assailed him for many days. In all the ways that Jesus was afflicted we see his dying (i.e., "death"; Paul uses here a word that describes a process rather than the single event of the crucifixion). Jesus' dying went on all through his life.

Paul relates himself here to the death of Jesus. He does this in several ways in his letters. Christ has died for or instead of him, he has been crucified with Christ (Gal. 2:20), baptized into his death (Rom. 6:3), united with him in a death like his (Rom.

41

6:5). Such statements help us to understand Paul when he talks of "always carrying in the body the death (dying) of Jesus." Because Paul once died with Christ, he dies daily with him (I Cor. 15:31). It is not that he is continually in danger of death because of his missionary work or that he rejects the claims of his body through the practice of asceticism. It is rather that he never escapes affliction, perplexity, and the like. So also Jesus calls us to deny ourselves and take up our crosses (Mark 8:34). This is not something confined to the moment we become Christians but is part of the essential nature of living as Christians. It was the way Jesus lived, a continual denial of the self as important and worthy of consideration. This is a kind of dying which goes on all through life.

Paul of course does not deliberately seek suffering. It comes as he lives as a Christian and results in the life of Jesus being seen in him. There is a natural connection in the thought here, for Jesus' dying was followed by his rising again. When, then, Paul though afflicted, perplexed, persecuted, struck down is not crushed or destroyed (vv. 8–9), it is because the life of Jesus is in his life. Because Christ has risen, Paul can "walk in newness of life" (Rom. 6:4). He no longer lives, but Christ lives in him (Gal. 2:20). As there is a process of dying, so there is a process in which the risen power of Christ manifests itself in Paul's life. As a result of this, he is changed into the likeness of Christ(3:18). As long as he lives he is dying for Jesus' sake, so that the life of Jesus may be seen in him (v. 11). And this is true for all of us: There is no escape "while we live" from the process of dying, which is the denying of self until we physically die. That kind of dying is inherent in all Christian existence.

Equally inherent in all Christian existence is the presence of the life of Jesus within, but it is a life which is never to be shut up within but always to be manifested to the world. Paul does not die in his ministry to satisfy some inner urge for unity with a dying Savior but that the life of that Savior should be seen by others. The manifestation of the risen life of Jesus, seen in loving service, wins men to learn of the Christ who died for them. Paul certainly preaches Christ crucified (I Cor. 1:23), but one of the essential ways in which he does so is by showing Christ's life in his life. He cannot show this unless he accepts Christ crucified for himself, and this of course he has done. Both the death of Jesus and his life are simultaneously visible in the life (body) of Paul.

42

We expect Paul now to go on and say "You should be finding the same in yourselves." Instead he introduces a new and surprising contrast: "death is at work in us, but life in you" (v. 12). It is, however, not so surprising once we have understood the purpose of Paul's dying. It is not for his own gain but for the sake of others. Here we come close to what he wrote in 1:6 (see also 11:7). It is taken even further in Colossians 1:24 (this may not be by Paul), where his sufferings are said to make up for what is lacking in those of Christ and to be for the sake of the church. In a sense Paul's death is a representative death, just as was Christ's. But Paul's death is not independent of Christ's, as Christ's was of all other deaths. Dependent on Christ's death, Paul's dying wins converts to Christ and, more importantly in this context, it should bring life to the Corinthians. Christ's risen life, which Paul sees in himself, ought to be appearing in them. Paul's dying is not for himself but for them. Is it not logical that if Christ's dying can mean so much for us, Paul's dying and our dying should also mean something for others and bring life to light in them? (See 1:3–7 for the way in which suffering and comfort are transferred between Christians.)

Paul has been saying this in the context of his ministry to the Corinthians, yet what he writes applies to all Christians. In troubles and anxieties we Christians find that God lifts us up over them if not out of them, that in our dying with Christ his risen life shows itself in us and that as a result that same life appears in those, or at least in some of those, with whom our lives are involved. In turn we are helped by those others just as Paul found himself helped and refreshed in a deep and spiritual sense by his converts (I Cor. 16:18; Philem. 20; cf. I Thess. 3:8). This is a mutual process in which every Christian should be bringing help to others and be receiving it from them.

It is not perhaps possible to explain in simple rational terms this interchange of spiritual benefit between members of the church. It is linked to the conception of the church as Christ's body in which the members rejoice and suffer together. If not easily rationalized, it has been a fact of the experience of the church throughout the ages. It means incidentally that members of a congregation have as much to give those who minister to them as to receive from them. More generally it means that every Christian by faithfully enduring affliction builds up other Christians in life and joy.

At least a part of Paul's contribution to the body of Christ has been his preaching. It indeed landed him in all the trials he described in verses 8–11. But it was also for the sake of the Corinthians (v. 15), that life might be at work in them. Moreover if he preached he did so out of faith, he preached what he believed. He draws in here a verse from the Psalms (116:10), probably hoping thereby to disarm those who criticized him because he did not use the Old Testament enough (cf. chap. 3). The translation (RSV) of this verse of the Psalm is based on the Hebrew text, and it differs from what we have here. Paul quotes the Greek translation of the Old Testament (the Septuagint). He usually quotes from this version, for it would be the one his Greek-speaking readers would have had available.

Paul, however, goes a little further than merely quoting the Old Testament. By saying that we have the *same* spirit of faith, he joins the believers of the Old Covenant to himself. Both he and they believe because God's Spirit has been at work in them and produced a believing spirit or disposition. Belief leads to speech. If we genuinely believe something to be important, we will talk about it. Paul believed the gospel to be all-important, and he went around preaching it. If he had not done so he would never have been persecuted or perplexed, and the Corinthians would never have been given their hope that they would be raised with the Lord Jesus and brought with Paul eventually into Jesus' presence. This is not just a vague hope for the future. Already Paul has found the life of Jesus within himself (vv. 10–11), so he knows and the Corinthians should know the certainty of their future presence with Jesus.

In what follows (4:16—5:10) Paul is about to go on to say more about what the life with Jesus will be, but before he does so he cannot restrain himself from running on beyond his immediate objective to his ultimate: Everything that happens is for the glory of God. The Greek here is difficult, and we may either take it as here (in the RSV) of the extension of the church in numbers or as in some other translations (e.g., AV) of the growth of the majority in the depth of their faith. Whether more join the church or each member grows in grace, all will increase their thanksgiving to God, from whom everything derives, and this will be to his glory.

II Corinthians 4:16—5:10
Hope in the Face of Death

Paul picks up again what he had said in verse 1, ". . . we do not lose heart." What he wrote in between was not however parenthetical. It contained a number of contrasts between the weakness of his daily life and the ultimate source of that life, God. Paul now gives a new twist to this by contrasting present life with life after death and sketching the nature of that life. In it lies his hope.

When he contrasts inner and outer natures Paul does not have in mind the comparison common in the ancient world as in ours of an immortal soul imprisoned in a mortal body from which it is set free at death. Nor has he in mind the contrast of the loss of physical vigor with old age and a possible deepening of life in the spirit. "Our outer nature" is the life we live among other people in which we may be persecuted or suffer in other ways (see 4:8–11). "Our inner nature" is the new life that comes into being with our relationship to Christ when we become new beings (5:17). Our inner nature is not yet perfect or complete; it will be hereafter; meanwhile it is being renewed and is growing every day.

Once this is grasped, persecution receives a new perspective. It is certainly real and cannot be shrugged off, but the area of human existence in which it takes place, our outer nature, is wasting away. Its effect can only be momentary. What comes after is "beyond all comparison" for God prepares for us "an eternal weight of glory." Glory belongs to God, and he alone can impart it to us. Paul has his confidence because he does not look at the things that are seen but at those that are unseen. What is "seen" is transient; what is "unseen" is eternal. Paul did not expect the "seen" to last for long. The Messiah would quickly return and the new age appear in all its fullness. Already, however, the new age appears in that "our inner nature is being renewed every day," so that if the Messiah has not yet come we do not need to lose hope. We now see the new age, though not with the physical eye. We see it in ourselves as our

45

Christian life takes shape, and we see it in the life of the Christian community. The "unseen" things are there but visible only to those whose inner nature is being renewed.

One of the "unseen" things is life after death. When we picture this to ourselves we are sometimes dominated by non-Christian ways of thinking. The Greeks thought of the soul being set free from every material constraint. Others have seen the next life in very physical terms, streets paved with gold and strumming harps. Paul does not deal here directly with these misconceptions for he had already given the Corinthians his basic teaching on the nature of the heavenly life in I Corinthians 15. What is important is the continuance and maintenance of the personality into the next life. Since we cannot think of life at all apart from the body, Paul says that believers will receive after death new bodies no longer physical in nature but spiritual. While not using that terminology here, the three images he employs are not unrelated to it. Imagery is necessary because no one has gone to live that life and returned able to describe it. We have to use pictures of what we know here so that by contrast we may realize something of what that other life might be. Pictures and images are never fully convincing, and we ought not to push them beyond their immediate application. Paul then does not supply us with a blueprint of the next life but only with hints about its nature.

His first picture contrasts life here as life in a tent compared with that of the hereafter which is as in a heavenly and eternal house "not made with hands." Paul may be picking up here a saying of Jesus which used those very words (Mark 14:58; the step from "temple" to "house" is easy, for Jews called their temple the "house of God"). Tents represent the insecurity of this life. They are destroyed when we die, but Christians should not despair, for new buildings await them in the heavens. There God will rebuild their lives in a totally secure and permanent manner.

The second picture is tied in with the first but is in terms of clothing rather than housing. To pass from this world to the next is like the putting off and putting on of clothes. Is there a moment when we are without clothes and "naked"? What would happen if Paul died before Christ came back? Would he be out of action, so to speak, for the period between? Such a prospect would lead him to "sigh with anxiety." Paul is happy here carrying out God's work, even though he has many trou-

46

bles and trials to bear. He would rejoice yet more to receive his "new clothes." He does not answer here his own doubts about the interim, doubts probably caused by his metaphors. We know however that he thought the matter through and lost any hesitations he may have had. For in a later letter to the Philippians when he is in prison and faced with almost certain death before the parousia he writes "For to me to live is Christ, and to die is gain" (1:21). But even in our letter Paul does not allow possible doubts about the interim to prevent him from ending on a note of triumph. There are those who groan because they believe that death swallows up everything, the good as well as the bad, the mortal disappears for ever. For Paul what is mortal is swallowed up by life, eternal life. For this God has prepared the new garment, and as a "guarantee" (see on 1:22 for the word) that Paul will some day wear it he has already given him the first installment, the Spirit.

In verse 6 Paul introduces his third image, that of being away from or with the Lord. It is an easily understood image; it was used in the contemporary world where people thought of living after death with the great ones of the past like Socrates. From the beginning Christians used it; Paul's earliest letter has it (I Thess. 4:17). It does not, however, mean that Christians are deprived of the Lord while they live on earth. They have been united with Christ in a death like his (Rom. 6:5); they have been baptized into him (Rom. 6:3; Gal. 3:27) and are in him; he lives in them (Gal. 2:20). When, then, Paul writes of his desire to depart and be with Christ, he is not denying that he is with Christ now but is using "with" in a different way. To be "with Christ" in this sense is to be "at home with" him (v. 8). There is partial fellowship for Paul with Christ now, but there will be full fellowship when he dies. It is a case now of walking by faith; then he will have full sight. The unbeliever walks (i.e., "lives, behaves") by neither faith nor sight. Paul saw the risen Christ on the Damascus road, but though he does not expect to see him again in that way on earth, he has a real relationship with him through faith. One day, when he dies, he will see him and see him even more gloriously than he saw him on that road.

This image creates no problem for Paul about what would happen at the moment he died—he would be with the Lord. There are some who are still perplexed by what happens at the moment of death—is there a bodiless period between death when bodies of flesh and blood are lost and the general resur-

47

rection when new spiritual bodies are received? We have seen how the difficulty was created for Paul by his use of metaphors. When however he approached the matter from a different angle (we might call it that of spiritual experience, the contrast of faith and sight, or of being at home in the body or at home with the Lord); another and more satisfying solution appeared. The problem exists because the time sequence in which we order events does not hold necessarily for God. From our temporal angle if death precedes the parousia we are forced to ask what happens in the period between the two since we associate resurrection with the parousia. The parousia and the general resurrection, however, are both eternal as well as temporal events. From the eternal perspective the time differential does not count, and the logic of Christian thought and experience indicates that we are immediately and fully with Christ. The fear of any state of nakedness should then disappear.

As Paul explains his idea of the afterlife we appear to have drifted away from the main drive of his argument—the defense of his ministry. To this he now returns and in doing so picks up an essential question created by the idea of being with Christ: If Paul has partially failed in his apostolate, how can he ever be with Christ? Will Christ not reject him? Paul is not worried by the possibility of total rejection (though see I Cor. 9:27). Nor is he concerned with how unbelievers will be judged—elsewhere he speaks of a universal judgment (Rom. 1:18–32; 3:6; Gal. 6:8; II Thess. 1:7–12). What troubles him now is the thought of a judgment at which he and all Christians will appear. Their fate as Christians will not, however, be at stake. It will be instead a judgment on the way they have lived as Christians. So Paul writes (v. 9), "whether we are at home or away, we must make it our aim to please" Christ. It would be impossible to feel at home with someone whose wishes we did not attempt to meet.

Paul does not indicate where, if judged, he expects to be found to have failed. We all find it difficult to see our own failures (cf. Ps. 19:12; Prov. 21:2), and Paul is aware of this, for at I Corinthians 4:4 where the same point comes up he qualifies what he says by allowing that he himself is not the real judge of his heart. Only the Lord truly judges. At the parousia he will bring to light what is hidden (I Cor. 4:5).

48

Some Christians are unsettled or surprised that they should be judged for what they have done in this life (the idea is found also in I Cor. 3:10–15 and Rom. 14:10–12). It is important to note how Paul introduces it here: Not in the second person: "You Christians who do not behave yourselves will be judged," which might be taken as a threat. Since he is writing about his own ministry and his own intense desire to serve his Lord, he tactfully uses the first person. How could he expect to go scot free if he has failed? He says nothing about the nature of the reward or punishment to be expected for what has been done or not done. His language suggests a judgment to be made on the whole of life rather than a particular reward or punishment handed out for each thought or action.

Paul has been primarily concerned to write about his own ministry, but in writing about this almost all he says applies to all Christians. There is no special treatment awaiting apostles when they die, no special compartment for them in heaven. Verse 10 brings this out emphatically with its sudden use of "all." There have been Christians who have thought that judgment was not for them. Once they had trusted the Lord they could do whatever they liked. That that is not so is brought out by Paul in two different ways. First, as here, by emphasizing judgment; secondly, as in verse 9 and again in verse 14, by stressing the need for a proper response to God's love. This is seen above all when he sums up the argument of the first sections of Romans with their emphasis on the way God has acted to save by continuing, "I appeal to you therefore, brethren, by the mercies of God, to present your bodies as a living sacrifice ..." (12:1). He goes on then to outline the conduct Christ wishes from his followers.

II Corinthians 5:11—7:4
The Ministry of Reconciliation

We have just seen Paul view his ministry in terms of judgment. He now continues to defend it, and in doing so, enters into its nature—it is a ministry in which he brings to all people the good news that God reconciles them to himself (5:16–21). To prepare for this, he first shows that he can only understand himself and what he does in terms of Christ (5:11–15) and follows that by briefly detailing his actual behavior (6:1–10); he

49

concludes by re-affirming his love for the Corinthians (6:11–13; 7:2–4). Within this section 6:14—7:1 is a strange and unrelated parenthesis.

The Preacher's Motive (5:11–15)

Like every Christian, Paul will one day be judged by Christ. He is not afraid for he knows "the fear of the Lord" and has always lived as one conscious of judgment. If the Corinthians realize that he takes judgment seriously, they will also realize that he exercises his ministry as God wants it to be exercised and not in the selfish behavior for which some have criticized him. If he has persuaded the Corinthians to become and remain Christian, he has done so responsibly. Since as Christians they are able to judge for themselves ("your conscience"; see 4:2 for the word), they ought to accept him and be satisfied with the way he discharges his ministry. He has however no intention of boasting about what he has done. If there is to be any boasting, the Corinthians should be doing it for him. But for this to happen they need to know the facts. The "facts" include not only the details of his travels, his miracles, his sufferings, but above all that he will be judged by Christ and that Christ's love controls his whole life. These "facts" should make them proud of him so that they will be ready to defend him against those who criticize him.

The Corinthians knew what his critics had been saying; we do not. Paul takes it that his critics gave themselves a "position." They may have been rightfully entitled to their position as emissaries of James the Lord's brother or of the Jerusalem church or of some other church, but "positions" are unimportant. What is important is the "heart" which Christ will examine on the day of judgment. In chapters 10—13 we again encounter critics of Paul, though not necessarily the same critics as here, and learn more of their claims for themselves and accusations against Paul.

The way in which Paul speaks of his own ministry may seem over-confident here. Yet if he was not sure that what he was doing was right, could he have gone on at all? Almost certainly there will have been times when he will have had his doubts (cf. 4:8), but there would be little point in drawing the attention of the Corinthians to these. He has now made up his mind as to the right action to take, and he also believes that by and large what he did in the past was also right. So he steps

50

forward confidently. Dare we do the same? We often condemn those who come with a simplistic message in black and white and have absolute confidence in it. But Paul had thought his message through and it was never simple in the wrong kind of way; moreover he had backed it with his life. We can afford to be as confident as he was only when we have thought through our position as thoroughly.

If there are times when his way of life seems "outrageous" ("beside himself"), it comes from his devotion to God. So far as his behavior concerns the Corinthians, he acts as one in his right mind. He may talk in tongues (see I Cor. 14:2,9,14) or have a vision (II Cor. 12:2–5), but if so these are private religious experiences and not essential parts of his ministry. When Paul preached to the Corinthians, visited them, or wrote to them, he acted rationally, soberly, and sensibly. He is then a person worthy of their confidence, and he has behaved in this fashion often enough for them to be proud of him.

This brings Paul to the real controlling force in his life: the love of Christ. Fear may make us do what another demands, but it never affects conduct in the same basic way as does love. Those who are loved (and "the love of Christ" is Christ's love for Paul) will love both those who love them and others (cf. I John 4:19). Yet if love is to control it must have power. Love is often thought of as powerless. The cross betrays weakness (I Cor. 1:18–25). But love has a power of its own which is not to be measured in terms of ordinary strength or force. It enables martyrs to endure, women to abide overbearing husbands, and husbands nagging wives. The controlling power of love is not, then, the wrong kind of restraint or force.

Having introduced Christ's love Paul cannot but go on to voice what is both its greatest act and his own deepest conviction: Christ died for all. It is a simple statement and many have found it enough to live by. Scholars, however, have discussed it long and deeply without reaching any final agreement as to its meaning. That Christ died for all (Paul probably means all human beings rather than just all Christians) was a basic tenet of early Christianity and of all Christianity since (see Gal. 2:20; I Thess. 5:10; Rom. 5:6–8; 14:15), but what does "for" mean? If it means Christ died as our substitute, then we would expect the verse to continue "therefore all live." If it means Christ died to benefit us, what follows is again the wrong conclusion. This is true also if we think of martyrs who die for a cause. Perhaps

51

then we should look on Christ as our representative who dies for us. "Representative" is a word used in a number of different ways. Governments and businesses appoint representatives who act for them, but we never appointed Christ to act for us. Nor did we, as it were, elect him as our representative to vote for us in some assembly (he voted; therefore all voted). There is no sense in which we can be said to have commissioned Christ to die for us. He did so out of love while we were yet sinners (Rom. 5:8). More probable than any of these suggestions is the idea of our participation in his death. As we participated in Adam's sin, so we participate in Christ's act of righteousness and love (Rom. 5:12–19). Christ would then be our representative in a similar way to that in which Paul supposes Adam to have been. We shall see when we come to verses 16–21 that we again move in a similar world of ideas.

The final verse, verse 15, moves from Christ's death to our life in a way that causes no problems of interpretation, though there are many in the way we live it out. Christ's death requires a deep and abiding response on our part, a response that we can make because Christ not only died but was raised for our sake. We live by his life, and his love then controls us. Paul does not indicate the areas in our living where our response should appear, for there is no area in which it should not be present. Each of us has to work this out individually. Paul started off with a defense of his own position and with personal statements, but he rapidly drew in Christ and his sacrifice, and then the Corinthians. Good pastors always have those for whom they are responsible in the center of their minds, and though they begin with themselves, they end via Christ with others. This is what it means to be controlled by the love of Christ.

The Preacher's Message (5:16–21)

This is one of Paul's greatest passages in which, after affirming what Christ means to him (vv. 11–15), he goes on to trace out the nature of his ministry. Seeing Christ in a new way has given him a new understanding of ministry. This passage is so packed with vital theology that every verse in it requires careful attention.

Verses 16 and 17 are consequences of verses 14 and 15 (note the two "therefores") and are parallel to one another. Verse 16a makes a general statement which verse 16b particularizes in respect of Christ. As a Christian, Paul sees everyone from a new angle, and in particular, he so sees Christ. This new vision has been working itself out since his conversion. The old way in which he saw people was "a human way." Paul uses this phrase (in Greek *kata sarka*) frequently, but in other places it is regularly rendered "according to the flesh" (e.g., Rom. 8:4,5,12,13). In our verse it indicates, then, not just an inadequate or limited way of looking at others, as though if we knew them better we would understand them better. Human judgments are not merely inadequate. They are also tinged with prejudice and bias. We make them with our own interests in mind. Since Paul's conversion and in the light of his conviction that Christ died for him, he thinks in a different kind of way, once "according to the flesh" but now "according to the Spirit." His judgments are now controlled by God's Spirit. We might hesitate to make such claims for ourselves, for prejudice and self-interest govern us too much. Probably Paul is not claiming that all his judgments are free of self but acknowledging that this is what they ought to be and in fact have been becoming increasingly since his conversion. Insofar as he takes seriously that he lives no longer for himself but for Christ (v. 15), a new spirit pervades all his judgments.

Having spoken in this general way in verse 16*a*, he suddenly throws in one of those puzzling little sentences (v. 16*b*) which crop up again and again in his letters. Why should he say that he no longer regards Christ in a human way? Perhaps he had been criticized because he had never been a personal disciple of Jesus or because his views on Jesus were not sufficiently spiritual. Whatever the reason he makes this tremendous affirmation: Christ is not to be subjected to human standards of judgment. These were the standards Paul had used prior to his conversion. Now he has other standards to apply.

Yet, is it not true that, judged by human standards, Jesus does not come out all that badly? Even those who are not Christian and have thought about the matter place him among the really great and good men of all time. That of course was not how Paul assessed him before his conversion, or he would never have thrown his followers into jail. But even if Paul had not been biased in that way, he would still only have regarded Jesus as a good man. His conversion made him see Jesus as wholly exceptional: "One has died for all; therefore all have died" (v. 14). This is a judgment made according to the Spirit and made because Paul knows the risen Christ. It does not imply that the

53

life of the earthly Jesus does not matter. If the earthly Jesus had not been the kind of person he was but had lived selfishly, considering only his own interests, he would never have been the risen Christ and the unique person Paul took him to be, the one through whom God reconciled the world to himself (v. 19).

Verse 17 gives us another consequence of the death of Christ for all: All who have died with Christ are now in him and have been made anew. It is an odd thing to say of someone that he is "in Christ." People are not inside one another. "In Christ" (also "in Christ Jesus, in the Lord," etc.) is a favorite expression of Paul. He uses it in at least two different, though not unrelated, ways. God redeems "in Christ," so in verse 19 God reconciles the world in Christ, that is, through what happened in his life, death, and resurrection. But Paul also speaks of those who have been redeemed by God in Christ as themselves being "in Christ." Here we have what we might loosely term "fellowship." This should not be taken in an individualizing way as if each believer was wrapped up separately with Christ. Christians as a group form together "one body in Christ" (Rom. 12:5). They have been given various gifts to be used for the good of all.

When Christ died all died (v. 14), but they were not dead and finished. They enjoy new life. Paul expresses this with an idea he draws from the Old Testament—God acts to recreate the world that has turned away from him (Isa. 42:9; 43:18–19; 65:17). The theme of the restoration of an original Golden Age is found in many cultures; it appeals to something in all of us which longs for a fresh beginning. With Paul, however, this longing is no longer a wish about a faraway future but a present reality. Through his cross and resurrection, Christ has already created his followers anew. Paul does not mean that Christians have been given new ideals to live by or that they will experience a slow moral change brought about by a new desire to be good. They would then be recreating themselves. It is God who makes the new creation as he made the first, and as, according to Genesis, the first was not a gradual process neither is the second. It took place in the death and resurrection of Christ. At that moment Christians became new people. That is the way God looks at them. They, for their part, have still to work this out in the actual way they think and behave, no longer living for themselves but for Christ. In some this happens more quickly than in others, but it is taking place in all, for all have been raised with Christ. Paul has something here then for those who say pessimistically, "You cannot change human nature." He would have agreed but would have gone on at once to say, "But God can in Christ." The operative words here are "God" and "in Christ." We are continually influenced through others; Christ lives and through him God influences us: ". . . the old has passed away, behold, the new has come" (v. 17*b*). When we or others are made new it is because God has acted; all is from him (v. 18*a*).

Paul has not forgotten his main theme, his own ministry, and he returns to it by referring again to the significance of the death of Christ—it reconciles people to God (see also Rom. 5:10; Eph. 2:16; Col. 1:20 for this significance). Reconciliation is the burden of the message of his ministry. If all have died (v. 14), all also have been reconciled to God, though they may not yet have realized it. It means negatively that sins are forgiven (v. 19) and positively that we become the righteousness of God (v. 21). Here Paul links up with the major theme of Romans and Galatians. The casual way in which he does so indicates he had already taught the Corinthians about justification. Reconciliation is perhaps an easier term to understand than justification, since unlike the latter it is drawn from ordinary life rather than the legal system. Because it is an ordinary term, however, we need to be careful how we use it.

It has a number of meanings. We reconcile two accounts of an incident, but Paul is concerned with reconciling people to God. We say, "After a couple of years I became reconciled to the situation (e.g., that I would never become rich)," but Paul is not suggesting that after watching human sin for a millennium God became reconciled to it and decided to overlook it. We speak of two people or two parties in dispute being brought together in reconciliation by a third party through a carefully worked out compromise, but God does not make compromises and who would the third party be? Certainly not Jesus though some evangelists present his death as if he were acting on his own to reconcile a wrathful God and a sinning humanity. For Paul it is always God who initiates reconciliation. We come closer to what Paul is saying when we recall those human situations in which two people disagree, but one, though annoyed by the other, refuses to retaliate and seeks by word and action to

55

win that other over. It happens sometimes when the child of a first marriage resents the arrival of a new marriage partner, but the new spouse seeks to gain the child with loving concern. So God seeks to win us, and he shows his loving concern in the life and death of his Son.

Paul emphasizes that God has gone into action over our sin. He has not just smiled sweetly and waited for us to come to our senses, nor has he simply hoped that given time we would change our attitudes. Paul expresses what God has done in two related statements: (i) "in Christ God was reconciling the world ..." (note the interchange of text and footnote between the first and second editions of the RSV; the second is almost certainly correct, for Paul is not speaking about the incarnation [God was in Christ] but about what God has done through Christ [this is what "in Christ" means here] to reconcile the world). (ii) "... he made him to be sin who knew no sin. ...." The second statement is intended to explain the first. It suggests the transfer of our sin to Christ. Christ who is sinless, in some way, is made sin; we who are sinful consequently become righteous. We met the same idea of interchange, though there between two human beings, earlier in the letter. In 1:3–7 Paul argued that his sufferings bring comfort to the Corinthians. In 4:12 he says that death is at work in him but life in them. Also related is 5:14: Christ lives, Christ dies; all die, all live in a new risen life. How can this kind of interchange take place? Are not a person's moral and spiritual qualities essentially their own?

The interchange of such qualities was a common idea in the world of the Bible and is still found in some cultures today. Within families the actions of the head of the family affect others. When Daniel was delivered from the lion's den not only were his accusers cast into it but also their wives and children (Dan. 6:24). We would not punish the families of criminals in that way. When the chief priest sinned, he brought guilt on all the people (Lev. 4:3). Such views went with the less individualistic conception of personality which was then held. Groups of people like the family and the nation were regarded as so much a single unit that the actions of the main member or even of any member affected all in the group. So the servant in Isaiah 53: 4–6 suffers for the transgressions of his fellows. Jewish writings later than those of the Old Testament continue to express the idea. In II Maccabees 7:37–38 one of the martyrs trusts that through his death God's wrath will be turned away from Israel:

56

I, like my brothers, give up body and life for the laws of our fathers, appealing to God to show mercy soon to our nation and by afflictions and plagues to make you confess that he alone is God, and through me and my brothers to bring to an end the wrath of the Almighty which has justly fallen on our whole nation.

Such passages help us to understand what Paul wrote in verse 14 and verse 21.

Though strange at first sight, it is a way of thinking to which we are not wholly unaccustomed. If a husband turns out to be a criminal, one of the contributing factors may be the atmosphere of his home; his wife may not then be entirely free of guilt. When the rulers of a nation make a decision, that decision is never purely their own. They would not be the rulers of the nation and able to make decisions if the people did not to some extent support them. Even dictators do not come to power unless there is something in the national ethos which is ready to accept them. Conversely good rulers have allayed evil in their nations, and good husbands (or wives) have influenced their spouses and children for good.

If Adam brought all human beings into the situation where they sin by poisoning the atmosphere of life with evil (we may not believe in Adam but Paul did), may there not be others whose goodness changes evil into goodness? And if there are such, and the story of the church, if not the whole history of humanity, is full of instances, may there not be one, Christ, who does this more completely and effectively than others? We may not be able to explain this in fully rational terms, but, like Paul, we can affirm that it works because we have known it to happen to ourselves and others. But we have also known those who are completely unmoved by it. What God offers in love may be refused and what Jesus has borne for others may be ignored. Many may not even know about it. So it is necessary that what Jesus has done should be brought home to them. A preacher is needed (Rom. 10:14), though not necessarily one who uses a pulpit.

Paul was of course a preacher. What he has been saying will have reminded the Corinthians of his preaching, for some of the phrases in verses 18–21 (e.g., "in Christ God was reconciling the world to himself") are probably drawn from brief statements of faith which would have been central to his original message in Corinth. If God has delivered people from sin through Christ,

57

he has also appointed those who should make this known. The one is as necessary as the other. Paul then in his ministry is a part of God's saving purpose. It was no passing whim of his own that brought him to Corinth; God had sent him. Paul describes his ministry with a term to which we are accustomed through his use of it (it had not previously been much employed in religion): He is Christ's ambassador (v. 20). Ambassadors have full power to speak for the government they represent and can commit it to a course of action. Since they have also often to reconcile opposing views and people, it is an appropriate term to apply to those who represent Christ. If we think of ourselves in this way, then we also need to remember the responsibility that goes with being an ambassador. In what we say and do, we commit our principal, Jesus. He will be judged by the way we live.

"The ministry of reconciliation" suggests the work of those who mediate—statesmen who bring together warring nations or counselors who seek to save a marriage. When Paul uses the phrase, he applies it not to the reconciliation of people with one another but to their reconciliation with God. In Ephesians 2: 14–17 it is used of the reconciliation of Jews and Gentiles, but this is based on the reconciliation of both to God. For Paul all true peacemaking between human beings entails their peace with God. Where they have that peace, it should be manifested in peace with one another. Yet we cannot claim peace with God unless we are at peace with our neighbors (Matt. 5:23–24). This may be the reason Paul tells the Corinthians to be "reconciled to God." As Christians are they not already so reconciled? They have not however always lived at peace with one another. We can see this even in First Corinthians (1:12–13; 6:1–6; 11:18). In our letter we have seen there were those who criticized Paul. He might then have said, "Let us be reconciled to one another." Instead he makes a deeper appeal, "Let us be reconciled to God." Their reconciliation with one another should then follow.

Paul has been looking at Christ's death as reconciling those who are separated from God by sin. Sin is still seen by many as that which separates them from God, but there are others who reject God or rebel against him because they see loved ones die slowly from cancer or made helpless as paraplegics through accidents for which they have not been responsible. Will talking about sin reconcile such people to God? If we look carefully we shall see that the basis of Paul's hope covers much more than sin. Jesus suffered unjustly. So did Paul. Some of what he endured is listed in 6:4–10; yet he always rejoiced (6:10). He may not have been a victim of debilitating illness, but he was sometimes rejected by those he expected to support him. He experienced natural disaster in his shipwrecks (11:25), and these must have hindered him in his main task of spreading the gospel. But there is no sign that what he innocently suffered ever turned him against God. In all he was upheld by God. The God of the cross is also the God of the resurrection, and Paul knew risen life already flowing through him (4:10–12). He looked forward to being at home with the Lord (5:6–8). And if in that life they do not marry or give in marriage (Mark 12:25), neither do they go about in wheel chairs.

The Preacher's Life (6:1–10)

These ten verses are closely linked to 5:16–21. In verses 1–2 Paul exercises the ministry of reconciliation of verse 18 and appeals to the Corinthians. Although the translation conceals it, verses 3–10 are tied grammatically to verse 1. They continue Paul's defense of his ministry. Those who preach reconciliation must themselves practice it.

In 5:11–21 Paul wrote about the saving event. This event includes his own preaching and writing for he works together with God ("him" in v. 1 can only refer to God). Paul does not proclaim this in any proud way: God and I are doing it together! A saving event which requires the conscious acceptance of those to be saved and was not made known would never save anyone. Paul has then a part to play in God's plan of salvation; this means he has now to entreat them. His words betray a touch of anxiety for he fears they may reject his gospel and with it himself. Just as there is a continual need to be reconciled to God (see 5:20), so there is a continual need to accept salvation day by day, "now is the day of salvation." No group of Christians can think itself so firm in the faith that it does not need to go back again and again to examine itself lest it accept in vain the grace of God, the gracious way he has acted in Christ. The same is true for the individual Christian. For the group the danger may be that of following some eccentric idea or leader; for the individual it may be that of drifting away from an earlier enthusiasm and an accommodation to a diluted form of Christianity.

59

The "day" then of which Paul writes is today, and it is a day which will continue until Christ returns. Often when people use verses 1–2 they apply them to unbelievers: Now is the time for them to repent. Paul however is writing to believers. Salvation is not an instantaneous event but a continuing process.

Now that he has exercised his ministry of reconciliation in the appeal of verses 1–2, Paul moves to a brief account of that ministry by sketching how he has lived and worked. Verses 4–10 are impressive even in English, much more in the original Greek, because of their rhythmic and lyrical style. This makes them difficult to analyze. It is also impossible to attach each phrase to some known event in Paul's life, and perhaps wrong to try to do so. It is better to feel the impact of the whole than to tie up the details. In this way the pressures bearing in on Paul in his mission are brought home to us. Under these pressures he runs the danger of putting obstacles in his converts' way. He believes he has never done this; unfortunately people imagine obstacles where none exist, and Paul has been criticized. Has he then caused the Corinthians to stumble? The whole intent of the passage is to demonstrate that any supposed obstacles are unreal. The good ambassador smooths away obstacles. If they are still there, then Paul has failed in his ministry of reconciliation and has not brought his converts to God.

So Paul describes his mission, even if that sounds a little like the self-commendation he elsewhere abhors (3:1–3; 11:16,30, etc.). Where false accusations have been made against the messenger and people turn away from his message, he must commend himself so that they may be won back to the message. Message and messenger can never be wholly separated. The character of the preacher must approximate what he preaches. So also must the character of church members approximate what they profess, and while they should not go round continually saying how faithful they are, there will be times when they will need to defend themselves.

How then does Paul defend himself? Verses 4–10 break up roughly into four sections. To the first section (vv. 4b–5) "through great endurance" is a kind of heading. Clement, a Christian leader in Rome at the end of the first century, in a letter written to the Corinthian church picks out this virtue of endurance in his description of Paul (5:5–7). Whether he personally knew Paul or not, he will have known Paul's reputation as it lived on after him in Rome. Paul's endurance must then have greatly impressed his contemporaries. The nine words which follow (three groups of three) spell out what he endured. There were external adversities, "afflictions, hardships, calamities." He was ill-used by his fellows, "beatings, imprisonments, tumults." Ample evidence for all these can be found in Acts (16:22–23; 13:50; 14:19; 17:5; 19:23–41; 24:23–27) and in II Corinthians 11:23–29. There were also the things he endured voluntarily: "labors," the hardships and fatigues which fell on him as he traveled because he could not afford any luxury and because of the way he often worked to support himself; "watching," the lack of sleep as he pushed on ceaselessly from town to town, working for his living by day and preaching when he got the opportunity; "hunger," little to eat and little time to eat what he had.

In the second section (vv. 6–7*a*) Paul looks inwardly at his motivation. "Purity" is not sexual purity but purity of motive. "Knowledge" is not theoretical understanding of theological propositions but deep understanding of what God wants him to do. "Forbearance" is the ability to suffer fools gladly and not to lose patience with others. In Galatians 5:22 "kindness" and "forbearance" are the produce ("fruit") of the Spirit. This may be why our translators (RSV) have capitalized "Holy Spirit" distinguishing it from the human spirit. The original Greek cannot make this distinction and it is probably better not to insert the capitalization. Paul is thinking here of the human spirit which is holy through, of course, the action of the divine Spirit. "Spirit" when referring to the human spirit is often qualified with adjectives or adjectival phrases, for example, Psalm 51:17; Isaiah 57:15; I Corinthians 4:21; Galatians 6:1. Paul is not here claiming divine inspiration for the qualities he exhibits, though this would be true, but that his inner being is free of any defects which would defile his ministry. The next phrase, "genuine love," gives the positive side (the same phrase heads the list of virtues Paul seeks in Christians in Rom. 12:9–21); Paul's love is not an outward show put on to cover the furthering of his own desires and self-interest but is genuine. Love without "truthful speech" would be a sham, and Paul does not use half-truths and diplomatic lies in his dealings with people. Finally in this section Paul slips away from the qualities he evinces day by day to the "power" of God which sustains him in them.

61

The third section, verses 7*b*–8*a*, is clearly defined in the Greek by a change of preposition (note the English "with") but is not so clearly marked out by content. Paul employs the metaphor of armor regularly (e.g., 10:4; I Thess. 5:8; cf. Eph. 6: 13–17). Here he is probably indicating through "right" and "left" that he is equipped both for the good and the ill that may come to him (in Greek, as in most languages, right and left are used of good and bad fortune). Whatever befalls Paul, honor, dishonor, good repute, ill repute, he has weapons for attack (a sword held in the right hand) and for defense (a shield in the left). "Honor, dishonor," and the like represent the opinions others have of Paul. Some have stood by him, but there have been those who have been extremely critical. Whatever they say, he will endure.

The final section, verses 8*b*–10, provides another set of contrasts. Beginning with the same theme with which Paul ended the last section, differing estimates of him, these contrasts go on to the double aspect under which Paul sees his own life, outwardly in trial, inwardly in joy. While verse 8*a* was general, we can feel in verse 8*b* the traces of Paul's present dispute with those in Corinth who look on him as an imposter in his claim to be an apostle. This dispute becomes much more evident in chapters 10–13. "Unknown/known" gives a different twist to the contrasts. Few Christians came from the upper crust of society (I Cor. 1:26–28); most of them came from the obscure and so would be "unknown." No one would have listed Paul in "Who's Who." His fellow rabbinical pupils would have thought his life wasted, his talents thrown away. It is possible Paul has a different contrast in mind here, that between the views held of him by the world and that held by God: unknown in the world but well known to God. With "dying, and behold we live," Paul returns to the theme of 4:11 and echoes it again in "punished, and yet not killed" (cf. 4:9). He had been punished many times by both Jews and Romans, yet not killed (Acts 14:19). Possibly we should take the first two contrasts of verse 9 metaphorically: People thought Paul to be no longer of any account; they wrote him out of their minds; he was as good as dead; yet he continued to live and to live in passionate activity for God.

In "as sorrowful, yet always rejoicing," two different moods into which Paul fell from time to time are contrasted. He had

62

been grieved by those Jews who continued to reject their Messiah (Rom. 9:1–5), by the Corinthians themselves (e.g., II Cor. 2:1–3), by the possible death of Epaphroditus (Phil. 2:27). Nevertheless, he can rejoice (cf. 7:4,7,9). He is made glad when his mission results in converts, when converts who have gone astray return to the faith, when above all he remembers what God has done for him and through him. Joy should indeed be the theme of every Christian life (Rom. 12:12; Phil. 3:1; 4:4).

In the final two clauses Paul again contrasts inward and outward. Poor by the standards of the world, he is rich in God's grace. Possessing nothing, as possessions are reckoned for taxation purposes, he possesses everything that matters (I Cor. 3: 21,22). Jesus promised his disciples that though they might have to give up not only money and possessions but even families and dear ones, they would receive in the Christian community, as it were, a hundred new families (Mark 10:29–30). The spiritual riches of the new community, the church, far exceed those of the best of existing communities, the family. In all these contrasts of the final section we come close to the spirit of the Beatitudes (Matt. 5:3–12; Luke 6:20–23).

Paul has sketched the ideal of the Christian life as exercised to help others and has claimed to fulfill it. For the passage to make its full impact on us, we should re-read it with every "we" replaced with "I" and in its light re-examine our lives. If we wish to preach it, we should be summoning others to re-read it in the same way.

The Preacher's Love for His People (6:11–13; 7:2–4)
(For discussion of 6:14—7:1 see next section.)

Paul now ends the discussion of his ministry which has occupied him since 2:14 and in doing so reaffirms ("said before," 7:3) his love for the Corinthians. We should not read too much into "to die together and to live together," for similar phrases appear regularly in Greek literature to denote close affection. There is thus no deep reference here to dying and rising with Christ. If death and life cannot separate Paul from Christ's love, no more can they separate the Corinthians from Paul's love. Paul therefore cannot have taken any advantage of them (7: 2*b*). He has not even extracted fees from them for his preaching as did many wandering teachers and philosophers (see on 11: 7–9).

63

His love for them has enabled him to speak freely to them; this is what the phrase "our mouth is open" means, not that his tongue has run away with him so that he said things he should not have said. There has been no reserve on his part; he has neither held back relevant matters nor only hinted vaguely at them but has always spoken his mind. And of course this is the way he wants them to behave towards him (6:13*b*; 7:2*a*). They are his children in the faith, for it was through his preaching that they became Christians. (The reference to children is not to suggest that he uses "baby talk" with them.) There ought to be a mutual affection in which they trust one another unreservedly. Above all there should be no recriminations.

Paul might have pointed out their faults as they have either pointed out his or listened too eagerly to those who did. He does not intend to. He has great confidence in them for he knows they will endure as Christians. He is proud of them and expresses that pride to others (7:14; 8:24; 9:2–4). That he can boast about them demonstrates that their relationship with him is one that brings him comfort. Afflictions inevitably come, but the faith of the Corinthians brings him overflowing joy (cf. I Thess. 3:6–8). Since Paul does not expect the Corinthians to be perfect, he can rejoice in the measure of faith he finds in them.

Since at other times Paul speaks harshly to them, he might be thought now to be open to the accusation of practicing flattery. There is however nothing unusual in someone alternating praise and blame in seeking to win others to a new way of conduct. No one's behavior is entirely good or evil; it is therefore always subject to both praise and blame. If 7:4 and 7:5 belong to the same letter, the reference here to praise leads suitably into the account of how Paul received Titus' good news about the Corinthians.

We have now come to the end of Paul's defense of his ministry. It may have been a diversion, but it has brought us some wonderful passages in his writing and an insight into his care for his converts that we might not otherwise ever have had. It can thus form both the standard for an examination of ourselves, as we exercise our ministry of whatever type it is, and the basis on which we exhort others to the responsible exercise of their pastoral care.

FRAGMENT

II Corinthians 6:14—7:1
Be Separate

This passage deals with the relation of believers and unbelievers. It raises many critical questions as to its place in the
letter and its Pauline nature. For our purposes these may be
safely left aside. For their detailed discussion see the lengthier
commentaries. We shall treat the passage as if it was by Paul,
though this is by no means certain. In any case we should note
that the chapter division here is certainly incorrect.

Paul speaks of the mismating (literally "yoking together" as
with animals) of Christians and others. This was quite a problem
for new converts. They had come from backgrounds in which
no deity demanded exclusive worship from his or her devotees.
There were many gods in which to believe and each person
could choose to take a particular interest in one or, usually,
more of them. There was no reason at any time to limit the total
number which could be worshiped. It was therefore all too easy
for converted pagans to fail to realize the exclusive claim of the
new God, whom as Christians they now worshiped, and to continue some allegiance to their former gods alongside their new
devotion to Christ.

It was also very easy to appear to remain involved in idolatry since religion penetrated every area of life. Paul had earlier
counseled the Corinthians how far they might go in the use of
food that had been sacrificed to idols. A great part of what was
available for purchase in the marketplace had indeed been so
sacrificed. If Christians bought this, were they committing idolatry? Could Christians take part in festive meals held in temples
(I Cor. 8:7–13; temples were often used as halls for public functions) or eat sacrificial food in a friend's house (I Cor. 10:23–30)?
Paul had dealt only with the issue of sacrificial food, but it is not
difficult to see how other issues would arise. If a Christian was
a partner with a pagan in business and prior to some new venture the partner wished to read the omens or have a horoscope
cast, what should the Christian do? If a bad harvest threatened

and the neighborhood decided to placate the local deity with sacrifices, could the Christian easily stand apart from community involvement?

With this in mind we can return to the passage. Paul asks five rhetorical questions to each of which he expects a "no" in answer. In doing so he employs five synonyms (partnership, fellowship, accord, common, agreement) and sets in opposition two groups or two ideas. The whole structure of verses 14–16 with its skillful repetition serves to drive home the distance that should exist between Christians and pagans. If believers are becoming the righteousness of God through the death of Christ (5:21), they cannot associate with iniquity and must choose between idols and Christ.

Taking up the idea of the temple of God (i.e., the church) from the final question, Paul now moves to the positive side of what he has to say and does so through a chain of scriptural references (see RSV footnotes for their identification). The particular passages Paul has in mind cannot all be tied down precisely. Note that in respect to verse 16*b* the footnote in the Revised Standard Version correctly gives a string of references of which Paul has conveyed the general sense without using the exact words of any one text. The Corinthians may in theory have left paganism upon conversion, but Paul knows its prevailing power and that they must never cease cleansing themselves from its defilements. As they separate from that paganism, God will receive them as a father receives his children. In the New Testament believers are regularly termed "sons of God." Unusual here is the reference to "daughters." Paul appears to stress it deliberately. God loves all, and so does Paul. This care for all comes out also in his use of "beloved" (he usually calls his converts "brothers"). Though an accurate rendering of the Greek, this is an awkward word in English. "My very good friends" is weak but is probably the nearest equivalent.

It is perhaps a little surprising to see Paul write about the defilement of the spirit. We can easily imagine how new converts might be defiled in other ways through contact with paganism. Are we to think of wrong sexual thoughts? More probably of pride and self-righteousness. These might grip those who succeeded in separating themselves from outer contact with idolatry when they became pleased at their own success in forsaking their old ways. There are deeper threats to holiness than outward sin.

This passage raises quite a number of issues. First, it is not a prohibition against one group of Christians cooperating with another. It has often been used in this way, though when pressed the group which has stood apart has usually simply defined itself as Christian and all others as unbelievers. It is all too easy to draw up definitions which refuse the name of Christ to groups we suspect. On one occasion Jesus' disciples rebuked a man who was not one of them for exorcising in the name of Jesus, only to be themselves rebuked by Jesus (Mark 10:38–40). We should be wary then of applying our passage to those who say they are Christians but do not have the experience we may have had or believe precisely as we believe. Secondly, our passage differs from many others which demand that Christians should refrain from pagan sins (e.g., I Cor. 6:18; 10:14; Rom. 13:12–13) in that it demands dissociation from people. Thirdly, the passage is not a direct attack on mixed marriages (the word "mating" has suggested this to some). Indeed in I Corinthians 7:12–14 Paul discourages the breaking up of marriages where one partner is an unbeliever. When he criticizes illicit sexual unions in I Corinthians 6:12–20, he is not referring to marriages. Husband and wife are made "one flesh" in marriage, and this cannot be easily broken. As we have seen, paganism penetrated deeply the whole culture of the ancient world, and it is against that wide influence that Paul writes. Actual idolatry was present everywhere, and Paul is primarily concerned with it and not with the things we sometimes term "idols," for example, wealth, position, success.

Christians today in Western civilization do not see idols on every street corner and are in little danger of becoming involved in their worship through their association with non-Christians. How far though can Christians work alongside and with non-Christians? Should Christians work with Marxists to improve the lot of the oppressed? (Let no one answer that Marxists do not have such ends in view!) Should Christians employ non-Christians? (Christians are usually very eager to sell their services to non-Christians for financial reward!) Should nurses who hold abortion to be wrong assist doctors who carry out such operations when no other nurses are available to assist?

Behind these issues lies a deeper problem. It was easy for Paul to draw a rigid line between those who had responded to the claims of Christ and those who had either never heard of him or had not responded. Can we divide the world in the same simple way and can we be sure into which category we should place particular individuals? When we lay down definitions which say who is and who is not a Christian, we tend to forget Mark 10:38–40. Since Paul's day Christian attitudes have permeated deeply into Western society. Marx himself was a product of Judaeo-Christian culture. Shall Christians separate themselves from non-Christians whose ways have been affected by the Christian ethos?

Again what is the effect of separation on those who separate? Do they not run the danger of becoming Pharisees? The origin of the word Pharisee indicates that they were people who tried to separate themselves from others. They would have nothing to do with those they took to be unclean. Those, then, who attempt separation must be continually on their knees praying for God to preserve them from judging their neighbors and to deliver them from any feeling that they are the chosen ones and superior to others.

CONTINUATION OF PART ONE

II Corinthians 7:5–16
Paul's Joy

We now pick up again the story of the visit of Titus to Corinth, which we left at 2:13. Either Paul broke off the story there to take up the subject of his own ministry, or someone editing his letters inserted 2:14–7:4 from another letter. Verbal links can certainly be drawn between 7:2–4 and our section, but there is also undoubtedly a sudden change of subject at 7:5. What was said in chapter 2 is now partly repeated, and we are given additional information. In particular we discover there was an individual offender with whom after some delay the Corinthian church has now dealt. The church itself is repentant over its previous failure to act and in consequence the stress under which Paul was laboring has been removed. The nature of repentance is the main theme of the section (vv. 8–13*a*) to which are added brief introductory (vv. 5–7) and concluding (vv. 13*b*–16) paragraphs.

Titus and Paul Meet (7:5–7)

In 2:12–13 we saw that Paul had been so worried about the situation in Corinth and the delayed return of Titus that he had left his evangelistic work in Troas to go to Greece to meet him. Crossing over then to Macedonia, he hoped to be comforted by the churches there (those of Philippi, Thessalonica, Beroea). Unfortunately these had been suffering persecution ("fighting without") or some other trouble coming from outside. There may also have been internal trouble ("fear within") in one or another of them. That Paul refers to affliction does not mean that he suffered physically, though of course mental worry can have physical effects. Whatever was wrong it did not help to allay his uneasiness about what might be happening in Corinth. This uneasiness had come about because he had changed his plans about visiting that city, had written a letter and sent a substitute, Titus. He is afraid that though he had done it all in good faith, he may have misread the Corinthian situation and only made things worse.

Eventually Paul and Titus met. Paul does not tell us when or where. Such details were unimportant compared to the wonderful news that Titus brought. Whatever had been wrong had now been settled. Paul need no longer worry. He sees God's hand at work. To express this he uses language drawn from Isaiah 49:13 (he uses the Septuagint; the Hebrew translated by the RSV is slightly different). Paul has been lifted up out of his utter misery ("downcast" is too weak a word).

When Titus left for Corinth he must have known that he was setting out on a difficult mission, but he accomplished what he had been sent to do and was comforted by the way the Corinthians had responded. Comfort spreads among Christians (cf. 1:6), and so Paul also is comforted. Three things had comforted Titus: (i) the "longing of the Corinthians" for the restoration of good relations with Paul; (ii) their "mourning" because Paul had been forced to stay away (1:23) and the realization that this had been their fault; (iii) their renewed zeal for the Paul whom they had been criticizing since now they recognized him again as God's representative.

It was not unnatural that Paul should feel elated by Titus' good news. His policy had worked. But he does not boast about that. We for our part should be careful, when disputes in which we are personally involved are resolved, that we are not more pleased by our escape from consequences we would not like than by their resolution. And we should see the latter not as a tribute to our negotiating skill but as the working out of God's purposes. It will be God who will comfort us with the end of the trouble, and it will be to him that the praise should be given.

Corinthian Repentance (7:8–13a)

The trouble in Corinth had been caused by one person. We never learn who that person was or what was the nature of his offense (it is just "the matter"). Apparently he had in some way injured some other person. Most commentators assume, probably correctly, that this other person was Paul himself (see 2:2–8). There had been an incident during a visit of Paul to Corinth (see section on 1:23–2:2). It was this which led Paul to change his plans in respect to visiting the city and to the writing of the "severe" or "painful" letter (see Introduction). Although there had been one particular offender, the Corinthians as a whole

70

were not free from blame, and the letter had been written to them as a group and not to the offender.

The memory of his letter seems to give Paul some embarrassment. This appears in the way he writes, for in verse 8 the grammar of his sentence breaks down (this can be seen only in the Greek). It is a common experience of people that when they get into difficult situations their speech and writing tend to become a little incoherent. Paul had written a strong letter. Once it was gone he worried if he should really have sent it ("though I did regret it"). But the result now showed that he had not been overreckless in writing.

Initially ("only for a while") when the letter was read the Corinthians were annoyed. Paul had exposed their folly in supporting someone (the offender) who was not worthy of their support. We all have been duped at times by those who thought they had the cure for all our ills, whether the ills of the nation or the church, and when they have been shown up as charlatans we have felt foolish. That is a "worldly grief." So also was the grief of Judas, though in a directly opposite way, for he took the true cure for all ills to be a charlatan and in worldly grief he killed himself. To feel sorry for or embarrassed by our mistakes and false judgments is not "godly grief." We are only feeling sorry for ourselves. Such self-concern "produces death" (i.e., eschatological death, which is separation from God). Equally it is not true repentance when we worry only about escaping the consequences of something we have said or done wrong.

The danger of severe letters or of telling people off verbally is that we may make the recipients of our letters and our scorn feel foolish. This will not lead them to godly grief. Paul was therefore right to be worried about his letter. That its result was godly and not worldly grief says as much for the depth of the Corinthian commitment to Christ as it does for Paul's skill and tact. Their faith allowed them to take a severe rebuke and to be led closer to God through it. Of course this also testifies to the way Paul had presented Christ to them and built them up in their faith, and part of his joy will have come from the realization of the soundness of their faith.

Godly grief is not itself sufficient. It should lead to repentance, the attempt to set right what has been done wrong. We need to do more than wring our hands and say how sorry we are for what has happened. The Corinthians had done more as verse 11 shows. Paul lists seven items to prove it. Their indigna-

71

tion against the offender had been aroused and they had punished him. They have also been able to clear themselves of full responsibility, perhaps pleading extenuating circumstances of which Paul had not been fully aware when he wrote. So they had demonstrated that they were guiltless in the affair.

We regularly talk about repentance, deeming it part of the process of conversion leading to salvation. Paul speaks of it surprisingly rarely, only here, in 12:21, and in Romans 2:4. He links it to salvation but not as a preliminary to individual conversion; the Corinthians have already been saved in that respect. Salvation in verse 10 has an eschatological sense; as such not all the converted will necessarily attain it (Phil. 2:12; I Cor. 9:27; II Cor. 13:5). To attain salvation, continual repentance is necessary, and thus, repentance is not just the way we enter the Christian life but is an ongoing part of it. Possibly Paul avoided the frequent use of the word to express this because in Greek culture it was generally understood as a change of mind. His Jewish faith however had taught him that the whole being and not the mind alone needed to be involved. He also may have avoided the term because of a desire to give a positive orientation to the Christian life. Where there is constant prayer, rejoicing, and loving repentance will take care of itself and the danger of morbid introspection will disappear. It can be harmful if we dwell too much on our personal sins. Yet if some particular sin has been isolated and something needs to be done about it, as in this case in Corinth, it is appropriate to introduce the idea of repentance and stress it.

The Joy of Titus (7:13b–16)

Verse 13 is one of those unfortunate places where the verse division was done ineptly when divisions were originally inserted. Therefore this section commences with verse 13b. Paul has been relieved not only to learn of the success of his letter to Corinth, but he is even happier to see the joy Titus showed upon his return from his visit there. Titus can hardly have set out with much expectation of a warm welcome, for he would have been aware of Paul's anxiety about what was going on. However, Paul's severe letter was well received. How much of this was due to Titus' own diplomatic skill we shall never know. He can hardly have been an idle bystander in whatever discussions went on. He also had another difficult task, to raise the question of the collection (see chapters 8,9). It takes tact to ask for money where there has been unpleasantness!

Paul concludes this section of his letter with a renewed affirmation of his confidence in the Corinthians. Both he and they are members of the body of Christ. As such they are bound to work along together. This had happened, and Titus and the letter he had taken had been received with "fear and trembling" (a set phrase which should not be taken too literally). Every minister and priest should be received in this way as representatives of God, but many others also act and speak in God's name to us. Do we so receive them? When we have done wrong do we willingly accept rebuke? And if in God's name we have to rebuke others, do we do it in such a way as to lead to their willing repentance?

PART THREE

The Collection for Jerusalem

II Corinthians 8:1—9:15

Introduction

Some scholars regard these two chapters as belonging originally to a letter other than that containing chapter 7. There is an abrupt change of subject at 8:1, but such changes are regularly made in letters. Since there is little which prepares us in the preceding material for chapters 8 and 9 and their subject is not taken up again in what follows they may be treated in isolation as we expound them. How we understand them does not then depend on the view we take about the editing of Second Corinthians. Some scholars claim that although both chapters deal with the collection, they come from two different letters. Again the acceptance or rejection of such a claim does not affect our understanding of the broader issues with which they deal.

The collection is for the poor in Jerusalem. Paul had willingly agreed to raise it when he and Barnabas had gone to that city to discuss their preaching to the Gentiles (Gal. 2:10). Paul mentions it in some of his other letters (Rom. 15:25–27,31; I Cor. 16:1–4), and Luke tells of its delivery (Acts 24:17).

There are a number of puzzling features about this collection. (1) In Galatians 2:10 it is said to be for the poor, but in II Corinthians 8:4 it is for "the saints." Romans 15:26 suggests that it was for the poor among the saints. Since our two chapters are not Paul's first reference to it in Corinth (cf. I Cor. 16:1–4), he does not need to identify the recipients precisely. Probably

75

most of the Christians in Jerusalem were poor, and therefore, either description would suffice.

(2) Were the Christians in Jerusalem poorer than other Christians? Jesus and his disciples had lived in voluntary poverty. As active missionaries they made do with the barest minimum (Matt. 10:7–9). The first Christian community followed their practice. Those who had property sold it and contributed the resulting sum to the common purse (Acts 2:44–45; 4:32–37). They would have been the more ready to do this since they believed the Lord would soon return and possessions would then become unnecessary. However, the sale of their assets and the immediate use of the money meant that their capital slowly disappeared, and unless there was a continual influx of wealthy converts they would not have been able to remain solvent.

(3) Was it then their poverty that led James, Peter, and John to ask for the collection? While that would be partly true, the church in Jerusalem may have looked on the collection also as a kind of acknowledgment on the part of the Gentiles of its own pre-eminent position. Paul probably initially accepted the obligation to raise the money because he saw the need in Jerusalem and was inspired by the love of Jesus to respond. Other reasons might have come into his mind as time went by. The collection became an excellent way of displaying the unity of the Jewish and Gentile sections of the church, which were in danger of drifting apart over the keeping of the law. It also secured Paul's own good position and that of his Gentile mission in the eyes of the Jerusalem Christians. Less probably he may also have seen it as the tribute of the nations to Zion which was expected to coincide with the final coming of the Messiah. None of these reasons is explicitly mentioned in our chapters.

Organized giving of money was a well-recognized Jewish practice. Collections were made for the upkeep of the temple and its services through an annual tax levied on expatriate Jews of the Diaspora. Local collections were also raised for the poor. The first of these may have inspired the way Paul organized his collection, though it was certainly voluntary and not a tax. Voluntary giving to the poor was however widely stressed as a virtue in Judaism. Acts 6:1–6 shows Christians had already accepted the practice.

76

Paul had brought the collection to the attention of the Corinthians much earlier. When he writes about it in I Corinthians 16:1–4, it is as an answer to a query from them. Here in 8:10 he says they have been contributing for at least a year. He has told them (I Cor. 16:2) that the easiest way to meet the need is to give weekly. After Titus had visited them and succeeded in his main task of delivering the difficult letter (2:3; 7:8) and dealing with the offender (7:12), he had apparently revived their interest in the collection (8:6). He may even have brought back their first installment. Paul is not, however, satisfied with the level of their generosity. What he has now to say about it divides into five sections by no means of equal importance for preaching.

II Corinthians 8:1–7
The Example of Macedonia

Having heard from Titus about the Corinthian generosity, Paul begins his appeal by telling them what the Macedonians have done. There were at least three Christian communities at that time in Macedonia: Philippi, Thessalonica, and Beroea (see a map). These despite being desperately poor and suffering persecution (see "fighting without," 7:5) have given most generously. I Thessalonians 1:6; 2:14; 3:3–5 show that the Thessalonian Christians had suffered for their faith. Paul also mentions suffering in Philippians 1:29–30 though it is not a prominent theme in that letter. Persecution was in any case endemic in early Christianity. The poverty of the Macedonian Christians was probably a part of the poverty of the whole province, which had suffered badly under the Romans. In a situation of general poverty the Christians would come off worst. Persecution and economic boycott would normally be linked. Few converts came from the upper classes. Small shopkeepers might find their trade going elsewhere because of their new faith. Many of the slaves could not be much lower in economic position.

The persecution and poverty of the Macedonian Christians had not, however, closed off their generosity. Paul, aware of their poverty, had apparently not at first asked them to contribute, but when they heard of the collection, they had begged him to be allowed to participate (v. 4). Once included they gave not merely what might have been reasonably expected but beyond their means (v. 3). They had not been either compelled or exhorted to give but had contributed of their own free will. The generosity of the Philippians had not even been restricted to the Jerusalem collection. They had also sent gifts more than once to Paul to assist him in his mission work (Phil. 4:15–16). It may be this is what Paul has in mind when he speaks of them as first giving themselves to the Lord and to himself (v. 5); he was the Lord's representative to them.

In the final issue Paul, however, does not trace the generosity of the Macedonian Christians simply to an awareness of the need of others. He sees it as the work of God's grace (v. 1). Here as in all the discussion he uses words which have strong theological overtones (see "The Collection: Concluding Remarks"). We note now that the word rendered "relief" (v.4) is the one which usually appears as "ministry." It refers regularly in Greek to menial personal service, for example, waiting at table, and is so used in Mark 1:31; 15:41. In Mark 10:45 it is applied to the way Jesus served us. What, then, the Macedonians have done in sending money to Jerusalem can be put on the same plane as what Jesus did in living and dying for us. Our appeals for charity are often based on humanitarian considerations; Paul derives his from the personal dedication of believers to God.

Once he has introduced the example of the Macedonians, Paul turns to the Corinthians themselves. Comparisons can be dangerous. If made too bluntly ("You ought to do the same"), they may only annoy those whose help is being sought. Paul avoids this danger by using theological terms. In that way he emphasizes what God has done for the Macedonians rather than what they themselves have achieved. When he turns to the Corinthians, it is again the divine dimension which he stresses. To give to the saints is as much a work of grace as any of the spiritual gifts *(charismata)* Paul mentions in First Corinthians chapters 12 and 14. Here in verse 7 he picks up faith, utterance, and knowledge (see I Cor. 12:8–11) to which he adds earnestness and love (see I Cor. 13). In particular if they love him they should do what he says in respect to the collection.

II Corinthians 8:8–15
Rules For Giving

Introducing the example of others in relation to generosity may serve to repel them rather than to open their purses so Paul makes it clear he is not setting up the Macedonians as *the* standard for giving. All he asks is that the Corinthians should come forward in a similar way and prove the depth of their love (v. 8). He is confident they will not fail because he remembers and tactfully reminds them of the enthusiasm with which they had begun (I Cor. 16:1–4) "a year ago" (see the academic commentaries for discussion of this phrase). That enthusiasm had unfortunately now evaporated, probably during and perhaps because of the period of strained relations with Paul.

Paul foresees that objections may be raised against his appeal. (i) The Corinthians may retort, "There are limits to giving; of course others give more but then they have more." Paul had already countered this when he mentioned the extreme poverty of the Macedonians (v. 2). Now he says that people can only be expected to give in proportion to what they have (v. 12). Possibly the Corinthians originally made large promises about their giving. Then when they actually measured the cost they found they could not meet their pledges and drew back altogether. If giving is to be in proportion to what a person has, that does not mean the same fixed proportion is for everyone, as is the case, for example, in tithing.

(ii) The Corinthians may object, "The situation of the Christians in Jerusalem (the 'others' of v. 13) is not too desperate; if we were badly off they would never help us" (vv. 13,14). While there may have been other reasons for Paul's advocacy of the collection (see "The Collection: Introduction"), he was in no doubt about the poverty in Jerusalem. It would however be pointless to create poverty in Corinth in order to ease it in Jerusalem. There was no danger of that. Paul is only looking for equality—equality, it must be said, in poverty not in wealth. The age in which Paul lived was one of scarcity, not abundance. In Romans 15:27 Paul adduces another reason for the collec-

79

tion: The Jerusalem Christians had shared their spiritual wealth with the Gentiles and could expect to receive in return out of the material wealth of the Gentile Christians. If he had wished to do so, he could also have referred to the church as the body of Christ: Where one member suffers economically all suffer, though not necessarily economically (I Cor. 12:26). Paul completes his discussion of equality with a very strange argument: the gathering of the manna (v. 15, quoting Exod. 16:18). No matter how much each gathered, each had enough. Those who gathered beyond their need did not have more for the more rotted away. If then the Corinthians cling to the more they have, it will not in the end benefit them.

We have then some rules for giving: Learn from the way others give. Give in proportion to what you have. Share what you have with those who are more needy. It is all neat and tidy and can be applied to many more areas of life than wealth, for we have also to give of our time and our talents.

Yet genuine giving never works by rules and Paul never kept the rules! There is no carefully balanced equalization in 4:12 or 12:15. The widow who gave her all (Mark 12:41–44) did not make herself financially equal to others, and she was commended by Jesus. So Paul drops a blockbuster into his neat argument, and it all blows up in our faces: "You know the grace of our Lord Jesus Christ, that though he was rich, yet for your sake he became poor, so that by his poverty you might become rich" (v. 9). Here is no careful consideration by Christ of the proportion to be given out of what he had and no expectation that in his need he would receive from those to whom he was giving.

Paul is not thinking of the actual poverty of Jesus' earthly life: a poor wandering preacher with no place to lay his head. He is not contrasting the poverty of the cow shed of his birth with the magnificence of the palace where he might have been born. Rather Paul is contrasting heaven with earth. Before his incarnation Jesus was rich in every way; incarnate he lost all. Paul does not say precisely what he means by this, for he is not writing careful theology but stirring up the Corinthians to fresh efforts by reminding them of the wonder of the coming of Jesus to earth, of his amazing sacrifice in becoming human. The best commentary on this is Philippians 2:6–8.

80

If Christ became poor that we might be rich, in what does our wealth consist? It does not consist in money or in power but in fellowship. In the Christian community we discover a multitude of new ties, new homes with new mothers, fathers, brothers, sisters, possessions, lands, and eternal life (Mark 10:29–30). Paul would have spelled out that final item as meaning the wealth of a new relationship with God through Christ realized in freedom from sin, in victory over the evil cosmic powers, and in the continual presence of Christ.

Paul does not spell it out here for he only wants to set before us the example of Christ, not to win our money by the hope of reward, even spiritual reward. The final standard of our giving is not to be the result of a careful calculation of how much will be left when we have given. Nor ought we to be thinking of how much we will receive from others should we fall into need. The only standard is the love of Christ. In the light of that can we hold back anything?

Paul however has not restricted himself to instancing the love of Christ but, as we have seen, has introduced other reasons for giving. He did this wisely, for he was more concerned to help the poor in Jerusalem than to ensure the purity of the motives of those who gave.

We note finally two other things about verse 9. (i) Faced with what might seem a minor problem, a congregation falling behind in its giving, Paul goes back to basics: the action of Christ. He takes as it were an electric drill to put a hole in a piece of paper. Perhaps that is a wrong analogy. There may be no such thing as a minor problem. When Paul asked for a little more in the collection, he knew that what was at stake was not just some widow's next dinner but the life of the whole church. For if the Christians in Corinth were unworried about the Christians in Jerusalem, it would not be long until there was no church in Corinth. There might be a group which continued to worship together, but it would have cut Christ out from itself. What does all this say to us about the way we in the modern church give? Do we donate generously for the upkeep and enlargement of our own local church property and causes and in a more miserly fashion to denominational and national church objectives? Do we contribute willingly to glamourous well-advertised causes and forget the crying needs of the inner city?

(ii) In verse 9 Paul expresses a Christology and does so in terms of the situation with which he is confronted: wealth and poverty. It is not expressed in the normal philosophical and

81

religious terms. Strictly speaking these terms also belong to and take their meaning from the situations and cultures in which they were originally used. The first Christologies (Jesus is Messiah) were in Jewish terms because the first Christians were Jewish. The traditional terms used in the great creeds and confessions developed gradually. They stand as a permanent guard against unorthodoxy, but there is also a need to express the meaning of Christ in words that those without theological education can appreciate. This was what Paul was doing when he explained Christ in relation to the collection. There are many situations today of which Paul never dreamed. How do we express Christ in their terms while remaining faithful to the centralities of the faith? How do we express Christ in a culture in which women have a position quite different from what they had in the first century? What terms shall we use to bring Christ into the situation of a middle-aged executive who has lost his job and will never get another? Should we say that the Christ who created and who sustains the universe (Col. 1:16–17) became a carpenter so that those without work or with unimportant work might reign with him in heavenly places working eternally? The possibilities of expressing Christ in terms of the real situations of people are endless. The risks of error are vast, but only experiment can show us where we can go. And proper experiments can only be made in the living situation as we meet people.

II Corinthians 8:16–24
Practical Arrangements

It is not enough to exhort people to give. It is also necessary to make arrangements for the collection and disposal of their gifts and Paul now turns to this. He is going to send three people to Corinth to accomplish this effectively. He explains who they are so that when they arrive with a letter (II Cor. or at least part of it), looking for money, the Corinthians may not be taken by surprise.

They already know Titus as one of Paul's personal team

who has previously visited them. The other two are unnamed. (See the commentaries for speculations on their identity.) One of them had been appointed by the churches to assist with the collection (v. 19). He was someone worthy of the task and well-known (v. 18), someone who, like Paul, had been involved in the preaching of the gospel. We do not know what group of churches appointed him; it may have been those in Macedonia or Asia or Galatia. More importantly this appointment made him independent of Paul. One peril facing those who collect money is the accusation that, under the pretense of caring for those in need, they have been lining their own pockets. Today competent outside auditing of accounts removes any possible danger. No such auditing was possible in the ancient world. Paul knew that many traveling philosophers and teachers in his contemporary world took advantage of their position to deceive others and to satisfy their own greed. At one stage he had apparently been accused in Thessalonica of doing this (I Thess. 2:5). He may already have been accused of it in Corinth (cf. 2:17), and he certainly was later (12:14–18). Whether or not he anticipated trouble, he takes care that one of those going to Corinth should come from outside his own immediate group of associates.

The third member of the team came from Paul's group (v. 22). He and the second member are termed "messengers." (In Greek it is the same word as "apostle"; used with varying significance in the New Testament it denotes here someone with a limited commission, probably in the area of finance; cf. Phil. 2:25.)

Paul hopes the Corinthians will give well, for the two unnamed brothers travel regularly and will report to other churches what has been given. Now is the time for the Corinthians to prove their love for the needy of Jerusalem and to preserve Paul from looking foolish because he had boasted about their generosity.

This passage may not take us deeply into theology, but it reminds us that love for others without proper planning may be disastrous. Part of genuine care for those in need is practical management—and this applies to all the church's activities.

II Corinthians 9:1–5
Be Ready When I Come

Attention now turns from the messengers to the purpose of their visit to Corinth. In the matter of the collection, the Corinthians (Corinth was the chief church in Achaia; see on 1:1–2) had begun enthusiastically, and in consequence, Paul had praised them to the Macedonians in order to encourage the latter to a similar effort. Unhappily his praise had not been sustained by events. The Macedonians had in fact outstripped the Corinthians in their giving (8:1–5). If, as is probable, some from Macedonia were to accompany Paul on his next visit to Corinth, both Paul and the Corinthians would be humiliated. To avoid this he has sent the brothers (8:16–24) to take up the matter and so ensure that the Corinthian contribution is both ready and a worthy offering. The word Paul uses here for "gift" is unusual. It is normally rendered "blessing." God blesses us and we can bless others. Here the blessing is not verbal but expressed in very concrete terms: money. Words of blessing come easily; to bless by sharing our material possessions requires quite another attitude.

In these two chapters Paul has stimulated rivalry between Corinth and Macedonia by setting up each as an example to the other (see 8:1–7 and 9:1–5). This may not seem the most Christian way to go about raising money. It may not seem right either that Paul should speak about his personal humiliation if the Corinthians fail (9:4). Against this we need to remember the very great importance Paul attached to the collection. It would both alleviate the poverty of the Jerusalem Christians and help to preserve the unity of the church. Here we face the perpetual problem of the end and the means. Is Paul justified in using what seem to be impure motives in order to stimulate the Corinthians? He has used the deepest and purest of motives in his appeal to the example of Christ in 8:9. He has added others over which we may stumble in theory though we regularly use them in practice. The Jewish Christians in Jerusalem must be made aware of the thankfulness of the Gentile Christians for the gospel and of their concern that none should go hungry or naked. Whatever we think of parts of Paul's appeal, it seems to have been successful, for Romans 15:26 suggests no dissatisfaction on his part with its result.

II Corinthians 9:6–15
Final Exhortation to Generosity

Paul has a few more arguments to put to the Corinthians before he comes to the climax of his exhortation in verses 13–15 —their contribution will be to the glory of God.

He comes near to saying "Give, for giving benefits the giver." There is a rich harvest for those who sow bountifully. They will never lack; their resources will be multiplied, and their harvest increased (v. 12). They will be enriched in every way (v. 11). Paul sustains this argument with Old Testament texts (see the footnotes of the RSV for references). What he writes is wholly in line with much of the Old Testament and contemporary Jewish thought. There are also sayings of Jesus which could be quoted in support, "But when you give alms, do not let your left hand know what your right hand is doing ... and your Father who sees in secret will reward you." (Matt. 6:3–4).

But is verse 11 true? Are givers enriched? In a famine area a starvation victim who gives her last bite of food to a child does not automatically receive more food; she only dies more quickly. The senior citizen who contributes beyond his means to a disaster fund does not receive any increase in pension. That I should have a passionate desire to end the poverty of the third world will not automatically enrich me with the necessary resources to do so (vv. 8, 10). Some commentators get out of the difficulty Paul seems to create here by saying that Paul is not thinking of a material return for generous giving but of a spiritual return now or in the next life. It is true that a giver receives a satisfaction that cannot be measured in material terms and that there is a next life, but Paul's language does not appear to exclude the material return.

We should take into account here what was said at the end

85

of the last section about the end and the means. Paul is so desperately concerned about Jerusalem that he does not think it wrong to bring into play the self-interest of the Corinthians. Note too that it is not his own self-interest with which he is concerned. If we put first the benefit to the recipients, we may find ourselves at times using apparently unworthy motives in persuading others to donate their money. It is better that they (this would never be true of ourselves) should contribute to a famine relief fund for the wrong reason than that people should die of hunger.

Verse 7 moves us away from what may have seemed prudential reasons for giving. In the first instance we are provided with another rule for giving: This should take place only after deliberate consideration of the need and of what the giver can contribute. So in I Corinthians 16:2 Paul had advocated systematic weekly giving. It is a good working rule but again is destroyed as a rigid guide by Jesus' commendation of the widow in the temple who gave her all (Mark 12:41–44). Spontaneous and almost irrational giving cannot be excluded from the Christian response to need. The second point Paul makes in the verse brings us back to the motivation of the giver: God loves a cheerful giver (cf. Rom. 12:8). Paul uses here a couplet from Proverbs 22. It is in the Septuagint form of the text but not in the Hebrew (and thus not in the RSV). It runs, "God blesses a happy and generous man." It is not an exact quotation, and Paul is probably quoting from memory. Cheerful giving is contrasted with reluctant and forced giving. Those who give out of self-interest to receive a reward here or hereafter are reluctant givers, for they act under an inner compulsion to seek their own good. There is no genuine joy, only a cool and calculating self-concern.

For Paul the two great commandments of love to God and neighbor are inseparable, so he moves naturally from talking of our response to the needs of others to speech about the glory of God (v. 13). Indeed the closeness of the two commandments is indicated by his use of religious language in relation to human giving throughout these two chapters. In verse 12 he uses another such word, "service" (*leitourgia* from which we derive our word "liturgy"). In the secular sphere it denoted the service which the wealthy might make to supply the needs of the community. In the Septuagint it was used of the service of the priests in the temple. To give generously and cheerfully to the

86

needs of others is then one way of worshiping God. It produces thanksgiving. The Greek is a little obscure here, and it is probably better to understand it as it is in the margin (RSV). This makes it clear that Paul is thinking of the Jerusalem Christians who will give thanks because of the generosity of the Corinthian Christians.

Paul has now brought us to the ultimate reason for generosity: It brings glory to God (v. 13). Christ became man (8:9) to the glory of God, so we give what we can to increase that glory. In practice we more regularly emphasize the relief of the suffering of those for whom we appeal than we do God's glory. This divorces the two great commandments and reduces our faith to the keeping of the second. If giving loses its origin and purpose in God and his grace, both it and our faith will shrivel and die.

When the Jerusalem saints see the Corinthian generosity they will thank God not only for it but also for the faith behind it. They have had their doubts about Gentiles becoming Christians, and a serious rift in the church had been possible. Paul had stoutly resisted every attempt to set Gentile Christians on a lower plane than Jewish (see Acts chapter 15 and Galatians). Now he hopes that once the collection has been handed over Gentile Christians will be accepted as true and full Christians by the mother church in Jerusalem. The latter will see the collection as evidence of the surpassing grace of God and will not only praise God for it but will pray for those who have given it (v. 14). So the unity of the body of Christ will be maintained and its members will suffer and rejoice together (I Cor. 12:26).

With the final outcome in view, Paul ends on a note of praise: "Thanks be to God for his inexpressible gift." His gift is in the first instance the money the Corinthians have given, for it comes from him, but behind that and more importantly is the gift of Christ which inspired it. It is this gift alone which is worthy of Paul's paean of praise, and ours.

Concluding Remarks

We can now summarize Paul's reasons why the Corinthians should contribute to the collection. There was the example of the Macedonians (8:1–5). God rewards the joyful giver (9:6–7). There was their love for Paul (8:7) and his possible humiliation if they failed (9:4). For them Christ has become poor (8:9). Their generosity would lead to God being thanked and glorified (9:

87

11–12). In Romans 15:27 he adds that the Gentiles have received spiritual benefit from Jewish Christians. Curiously he never speaks about the poverty in Jerusalem. If we had run the appeal, we would have shown pictures of starving Palestinians and sought in that way to awaken sympathy for them. Paul of course may have done this when he initially raised the subject, but he may have avoided this approach because it was not common practice in Greece to evoke pity for the poor with emotional appeals. Paul moreover has another and very positive line of argument. He gives the whole discussion a theological orientation. Although English translations do not always reveal it, he employs throughout a great number of theological words. A list of the words will reveal this:

grace *(charis)* 8:1,9; 9:14

translated elsewhere as "gracious work" (8:6,7,19), "favor" (8:4), "blessing" (9:8), "thanks" (8:16; 9:15).

ministry *(diakonia)*

translated elsewhere as "relief" (8:4), "offering" (9:1), "rendering" (9:12), "service" (9:13), and with the verb as "carrying on" (8:19) and "administering" (8:20). See also—notes on 8: 1–7.

glory *(doxa)* 8:19, 23 (with the verb at 9:13)

fellowship *(koinonia)*

translated as "taking part" (8:4) and "contribution" (9:13)

service *(leitourgia)* 9:13 (see comment there)

Paul thus sets the service of the poor in the service of God. We make our appeals on the basis of need, Paul on the basis of what God has done. Generosity then within the body of Christ (Paul does not deal with generosity to all and sundry) emerges from the relationship of believers to God. Both the needy and those who meet their need have this relationship and consequently stand in a relationship to one another. This and not merely human sympathy should govern their attitude toward one another.

We do not know what success Paul had with his appeal. It must at least have been partially successful since in Romans 15:26 he refers to the contribution from Achaia, of which Corinth was the chief church. Equally we do not know how the collection was received in Jerusalem. By the time Paul wrote Romans, he had doubts whether he would be welcome when he arrived with it (15:30–31). Acts 21:17–26 (cf. 24:17–18) implies he had to pacify the Jerusalem Christians by appearing to adhere to the Law. Things were never easy for Paul.

As we have seen, he suggested some rules to govern Christian giving. As a Jew of the Pharisaic party (Phil. 3:5), we might have expected him to encourage tithing. What he does say, however, implies he would almost certainly have rejected it as a general rule. Giving should be in accordance with what we have. For those on the bread line tithing could mean disaster, they themselves becoming objects for charity. For someone in the upper income brackets to say, "I have tithed, I have given enough" would be untrue. Legalism and generosity make ill companions. When indeed Paul presented a "reasonable" case for giving, he ended by shattering it with penetrating theological insight. No rule can govern God's love for us, and none should govern the love we offer in return.

Paul deals here with a very limited situation about poverty in the church and the need to preserve its unity. We, however, cannot confine our attention to those who are poor among Christians, though at times this will be a first call on our giving. The divisions within the church are so deep that even generous giving will not by itself create unity. Poverty moreover is a worldwide phenomenon. In every nation some live on or below the poverty line; in some parts of the world great numbers are never far from starvation. The problem is too great for spontaneous generosity of individuals or the church, no matter how extensive, to solve it. Such giving may ameliorate the immediate effects of the sudden crisis produced by a famine or earthquake, but it can do nothing to resolve the underlying and continuing problem of world need. Much of our effort must, therefore, go into the attempt to move governments to tackle it. Since their giving will come out of our taxes we will be contributing our share. Paul could no more have foreseen this need of governmental action than he could have foreseen our need to deal with slavery and the color problem in the same large-scale way.

The Christian response to poverty may also have to go beyond financial assistance. What is required in some areas is not more money but changes in the social and economic system. Gifts of money may only improve the lot of the governing classes without helping the poor; indeed the latter may as a result be further oppressed. Actions by governments cannot always be expected to work. When they contribute cash they may have something in mind quite other than the relief of the

89

poor. Often they are more concerned to support one another and the *status quo* or to act out of ideological theory than to meet real need. In such cases it may be that it is only the response of Christians that can bring real help. If Christian support is, moreover, really to deal with changing the system, that support may need to go to guerrilla and revolutionary movements rather than to the immediate relief of the poor. Christian help may also need to be channeled into the advocacy of cultural change rather than just into direct help. Advice for controlling the birth rate to prevent a steadily rising population where there is not a steadily rising food supply may be more important than the temporary though dramatic alleviation of poverty in a small area.

PART FOUR

Opposition at Corinth

II Corinthians 10:1—13:10

Introduction

In these four chapters Paul deals with only one subject, the opposition to his work that has appeared in Corinth. Thus there is both an abrupt change of subject at this point and also a complete change of mood. A new and fierce tension appears as Paul introduces himself as a "warrior" (10:3–5). Certainly the earlier chapters revealed differences between Paul and the Corinthians, but the differences were being overcome. If Paul rebuked the Corinthians, he did it in the hope of reconciliation. From 10:1 onwards he is in a fighting mood. No oil is poured on troubled waters. False views and policies are met head on and refuted. It is hard to believe, as some have supposed, that Paul stopped his dictation for a few moments at 9:15 and then resumed it in such an entirely different spirit. It is even more difficult to believe that after writing 9:15 he had a sleepless night troubled by indigestion and nightmares and proceeded the next morning to take it out on the Corinthians. He must have had fresh news about a deterioration of the situation in Corinth. If 10:1 was written directly after 9:15, we would have expected him to mention the source of that news. Would he also have left unchanged the conciliatory tone of the earlier chapters? In particular what he has to write in these final four chapters would frustrate his careful diplomatic handling of the collection. If then we assume Paul received fresh news about Corinth, it is easier to suppose it came after chapters 1—9 had been dispatched. Chapters 10—13 are thus part of one letter and chapters 1—9 of another. Some scholars who hold this view believe they were part of the intermediate or severe letter (referred to in 2:4; 7:8,12), which Paul wrote between our First and Second Corinthians (see "Introduction"). It is probably bet-

91

ter, however, to treat chapters 10—13 as though they were written later than chapters 1—9 (for discussions see the academic commentaries and New Testament introductions). It would then have been natural to attach them after those chapters. Their addition means the original ending of chapters 1—9 and the original beginning of the letter which included chapters 10—13 no longer exist. They were probably both brief.

In our chapters Paul's gospel and his position as apostle are at stake. Both (for Paul they are not two issues but one) have been challenged by some who have come intruding from other Christian communities. Since he intends to visit Corinth again (12:14; 13:1; presumably the visit already hinted at in 9:4) and would like to clear the air and restore his gospel and authority before he arrives, he now writes to prepare the Corinthians. Throughout he addresses the Corinthians themselves and not the intruders who were his actual opponents. For the possible identification of the latter see "Paul and his Opponents."

II Corinthians 10:1-6
The Weapons of Warfare

Paul launches his attack not just as a warrior but as a Christian warrior, for he has been impressed by the gentleness and meekness of Christ. He wishes to display the same qualities, yet this cannot mean that he should ignore those who are destroying his work in Corinth for it is God's work.

Among the criticisms of Paul made by his rivals was the accusation that he was full of courage ("bold") when out of reach but "humble" when present. The latter may not seem a serious accusation to us, but the Greek word rendered "humble" has the same double sense as the English. It can mean "obsequious, servile" as well as indicating that genuine humility which Christian teaching opposes to every form of pride. Paul's opponents will have used it in the bad sense, but he is happy to claim it of himself in the good sense, in which it could stand alongside Christ's meekness and gentleness. Paul wants to be humble like Christ but is afraid he may instead have to show boldness (v. 2).

His critics have probably also said that he was acting in a "worldly fashion" (v. 2; cf. 1:17 and comment there). Both in English and in Greek these words can have a bad sense, denoting sinful behavior. Paul does not detail here the precise accusations his opponents had made. They probably said he had intrigued against them behind their backs, had passed round slanderous gossip about them, had changed his mind and broken promises (cf. 1:17), had tried to silence criticism by imposing his authority (cf. 1:24), had feathered his own nest by his financial dealings (12:16), had attempted to sway people with empty rhetoric containing no real argument. They accused him, in fact, of using all the mean tricks of which politicians, including ecclesiastical politicians, accuse one another. They may also have attacked him from a very different angle, saying that he was too worldly because he did not speak with tongues every day or have visions and special revelations, did not spend enough time in prayer and developing his own personal spirituality; instead he was too keen to collect money to send to far-off saints in Jerusalem.

Since so much is at stake, Paul feels he cannot ignore criticism, but if he fights he will fight with spiritual weapons. The use of the metaphor of war in relation to religion is well known. In the history of Israel it arose originally in relation to the occupation and settlement of Palestine. One of the much later scrolls from Qumran is known as "The War Rule" and depicts an eschatological contest between the sons of light and the sons of darkness. The theme has been a favorite one with Christian poets and some of our best-loved hymns employ it. As he now uses it, Paul does not individualize or identify the weapons of the Christian warrior as is done in I Thessalonians 5:8 and Ephesians 6:11–17. It is enough to indicate that the weapons have divine power behind them (v. 4).

He continues the military metaphor with "strongholds, captive" and probably also with "every proud obstacle," a phrase indicating a high rampart or defensive wall round a city or camp. The strongholds and captives do not represent people to be overcome but ideas and opinions, perhaps even policies. Paul fears these may turn aside his converts from the wisdom of Christ crucified and the true knowledge of God to another wisdom and way of life. There is nothing here to tell us what his opponents' arguments and policies were (see "Paul and His Opponents"), but we should note that Paul claims to attack

93

them rather than the character of those who hold them. Too often in Christian controversy upholders of the faith have resorted to personal abuse of their opponents rather than attacks on their views.

The battlefield on which the war is to be fought out is the Corinthian community, and it is a battle for the community's life. Paul's attack will be concentrated on "some" (v. 2) who have criticized him. Even now as he writes, these critics are vigorously at work in Corinth, and he believes they need to be punished. He would probably have been more tolerant with his own converts, whom he regarded as his children (cf. 12:14; I Cor. 4:14; I Thess. 2:11), than he is with these intruders. Like any parent, he is indignant with those who disturb his offspring. On the other hand, he expects that the Corinthians, as his children, will once again become completely obedient (v. 6) and will not need to be punished. Paul gives us no idea what punishment he has in mind. Chapters 10—13 do not give us the impression that there is a large group supporting Paul on whom he could rely to enforce discipline, as he had been able to do in the case of I Corinthians 5:1–5. The culprit was on that occasion excommunicated. Paul is now more likely to find himself excluded if there is to be a decision by majority vote. For the same reason any attempt at public censure would have been ineffective. Although it may sound incredible to us, Paul may have been expected to threaten those who disagreed with him with physical punishment. There are several cases of this in the New Testament (Acts 5:1–11; 13:4–11). In Corinth some who had participated unworthily in the Eucharist took ill and even died (I Cor. 11:30). As in the name of Christ the sick were healed, so in the name of Christ Paul might condemn with a solemn curse those who persisted in sin (cf. Gal. 1:8,9). If this was how he expected to act, he would certainly not then have thought of himself as carrying on a "worldly war." To seek assistance from the civil authorities, if such had even been possible, would have been to act in "worldly fashion."

The fight against false belief and against those who disturb congregations has not ended. With what weapons do we conduct it? We will hardly curse opponents, but are our weapons always "spiritual"?

II Corinthians 10:7–18
Paul Commences His Self-defense

Paul moves in two directions as he begins to defend himself: (a) In the earlier verses he seeks to correct any wrong impression of himself that may be circulating in Corinth. (b) In the later verses he argues that his rivals should have no standards for themselves other than those God has set and should also work within the limits God has laid down for them. (The RSV places the main break in thought after v. 12; others, e.g., NEB, GNB, after v. 11.)

(a) Paul begins with an appeal to the common sense of the Corinthians. If they would only think for a moment, they would see they are being led astray (v. 7*a*). Paul's critics have been asserting that they are Christ's and either saying or hinting that Paul is not. Paul does not deny their relation to Christ—there have been many wrong-headed Christians—but affirms his own. What is at issue here, however, is not simple Christian existence (whether Paul was a Christian or not) but Christian authority. Paul's opponents may have claimed that in some way their authority came from their having followed the earthly Jesus, which Paul had never done. If so, Paul would have said that his authority came from Christ but in a different way—from his experience of the risen Lord on the road to Damascus (see I Cor. 9:1–2; Gal. 1:1, 11–17). It is, however, more probable that his opponents claimed authority because they had been, and as Christians continued to be, good Jews, for in 11:22 Paul counters with a claim to be as good a Jew. They may also have made claims about their spiritual experiences, for in 12:1–4 Paul tells of a vision he once had. Whatever their claim, Paul affirms that his claim is as good.

More important than the claim to possess authority is the manner in which it is exercised. Paul received his authority from the Lord, primarily for building up the church (v. 8). Paul uses here, and again at 13:10, a phrase drawn from Jeremiah 1:10 and 24:6. He likes the metaphor of "building" and uses it elsewhere. He describes himself as a "skilled master builder"

95

(I Cor. 3:10); others build on the foundations he laid. Spiritual gifts are for "building" up the church (I Cor. 14:12). At the moment he fears that his opponents are not building up the Corinthian community but destroying it. He realizes that in the last resort he himself may have to destroy, but when he destroys he destroys arguments (cf. vv. 3–5) and not people. To destroy false arguments may indeed be a way of building up people. True pastoral care often requires the unmasking of seemingly innocent and helpful arguments, although when we do this, we need to be sure that what we unmask are actually false arguments and not just ones to which we are unaccustomed. This is particularly true when we exercise pastoral care across the generation gap. Each generation sees things in a different way, and it may be that it is our vision which is inadequate and not that of the next generation or the past one.

When the talk is about authority, it is always difficult to avoid the impression of boasting. Paul cannot be sure he has avoided it (v. 8), but he is confident that in the end the facts will bear him out and that he will not "be put to shame." His opponents will be revealed in their true colors and his Corinthian converts will return to him.

Meanwhile there is one argument his opponents have been using about his exercise of authority that he can easily counter: His bark is worse than his bite (cf. v. 1). They say he writes tough ("weighty and strong") letters, but when he is personally present he is all honey and sweet words. His opponents were certainly correct when they said he could write tough letters; chapters 10—13 prove this as does his letter to the Galatians. Tough letters can sometimes have the wrong effect, and Paul is genuinely afraid lest his "toughness" should have frightened the Corinthians (v. 9). Tough policies may scare people and quell opposition for a time, but it is always only for a time. They never solve underlying problems.

If then there is no doubt that Paul's letters could be tough, has he also been weak-kneed when in Corinth? This can hardly have been true of the "severe" visit (2:1–2) when he appears to have been rebuffed and to have left in anger. But a different impression may have remained after other visits. When he told the Corinthians that his policy was to become all things to all men (I Cor. 9:19–23), this could have been seen as weakness. His actual physical appearance may not have been impressive. The earliest known description of him says that he was small of stature, with a bald head and crooked legs, in a good state of body, with eyebrows meeting and nose somewhat hooked, full of friendliness; for now he appeared like a man, and now he had the face of an angel (Acts of Paul and Thecla in *New Testament Apocrypha,* II, 354).

The last phrase suggests that whatever Paul's physical appearance, he was what we would describe as charismatic. His character was not weak. Perhaps more substance may have lain in the charge that "his speech was of no account." If his letters are anything to go by, his grammar went to pieces under stress. The same probably happened when he became excited in speaking (it has been suggested that he stuttered, and this would have become worse under stress). When to this occasional incoherence was added his willingness to work with his hands to earn his living (Acts 18:3; I Cor. 9:3–18; I Thess. 2:9; it was not thought proper in the Greek world for an educated man to work with his hands), some of his critics may have concluded that he was uneducated (cf. 11:6). He seemed to lack the superficialities of oratory (I Cor. 2:3–4), which again were the mark of an educated person. But education and the ability to communicate do not necessarily go together.

In reply Paul is clearly not so much worried by the accusation of lack of education as by the charge that he is a different person when he meets people face to face than when he writes to them. Once he appears in Corinth, they will quickly discover that the charge lacks substance. How much real ground there may have been for the charge in Paul's case, it is impossible for us now to estimate properly. But what of ourselves? When the person we wish to reprove is far off and we write it is easy to let our pen run away, we use harsh words we would never use face to face. It is also possible to write honestly, and then when present, to lack the courage to say what needs to be said. If it is difficult to write honest letters, it is often more difficult to be honest in personal encounter. It is also easy to use an official position as a shield when dealing out harsh criticism—a peril above all to priests and ministers. It is easy to rebuke a congregation as a whole and not to tackle individuals within it. This is true also for many people in "official" positions, for example, teachers, parents; the temptation is to fall back on the "security" of "position" and criticize rather than have honest discussion.

97

(b) Now that he has defended himself against one criticism,

Paul turns more directly to attack his opponents. This attack has two main prongs: (i) They commend themselves unduly. (ii) They have intruded into his sphere of labor. (A few translations, e.g., Moffatt, Knox, read a different Greek text at the junction of v. 12 and v. 13 and so have a different rendering. That of the RSV which is basically similar to the AV, GNB, NEB, JB is to be preferred.)

(i) Paul deals here with those who commend themselves, not as in 3:1 with those who bring letters of commendation from others. Those who commend themselves have no external standard with which to compare themselves. So they "measure themselves by one another and compare themselves with one another" (v. 12). Such a practice, already condemned in the Old Testament (cf. Prov. 21:2; 27:2), is a standing peril for small groups. No matter how sincere their members may be, they run the danger of thinking themselves better than they are because they are wrapped up in themselves and their own ideas. If that is a danger for sincere people, how much more for those who are not, and Paul certainly has doubts about the sincerity of his opponents. The Corinthians should receive only those whom the Lord commends (v. 18) and not those who commend themselves.

Paul says, of course ironically, that he does not venture to compare himself with people like his opponents. Since he has been commended by the Lord, he has a standard by which to measure himself that is not purely human. Moreover he has letters of commendation, the Corinthians themselves (3:2), and they are also the seal of his apostleship (I Cor. 9:2). Above all he has been appointed by God to minister to them. There is then no need to compare himself with others in order to see if he measures up to their human standards. There is indeed only one standard by which measurement should be made—Christ. Paul seeks to imitate Christ (I Cor. 11:1) and to manifest the life of Jesus in his life (4:10). This is the standard by which the Corinthians ought to be assessing both him and his rivals and by which we ought to assess ourselves.

These rivals have boasted apparently about the success of their own work in Corinth (v. 16), ignoring Paul's work in founding the church. At best all they had done was to build on the foundations he had laid (I Cor. 3:10–15). If Paul for his part were to go to a church founded by someone else, he would recognize that person's work and not boast as if it were his own, even if he did preach a few sermons in the place (v. 15).

There is not much to be said in any case for boasting (see "Playing the Fool"). If it has to be, it should be about the Lord (v. 17). Paul quotes Jeremiah 9:23–24 (already cited at I Cor. 1:31 where its detail made it more directly relevant) to confirm this legitimate form of boasting. Such boasting does not lay stress on his self-achievement but on what the Lord has done through him (cf. Rom. 15:17). Yet even such boasting must have its bounds (v. 13) and should relate only to the work done within the limits set down by God.

(ii) His opponents have intruded into the area apportioned to him by God, indeed into that allotted by his fellow apostles, for they had agreed that he was to go to the Gentiles (Gal. 2:7–10), and Corinth was a Gentile city. Of course Paul could never have gone to every Gentile city. He would have been aware of other missionaries working among the Gentiles in places like North Africa. Barnabas was now preaching independently of Paul. Probably then within Gentile areas another rule would have been needed: Whoever worked first in an area could regard it as his field. Thus Corinth is in the field of Paul, and Rome is not. When he writes to the latter church, he recognizes this and says that when he comes he will not settle down but looks to be sent on to other areas; he will not build on the foundations others have laid (Rom. 15:20). If this is the rule, Paul is right to condemn those who have intruded into his sphere.

Yet Paul allowed his assistants, Silas, Timothy, Titus, to build where he himself had laid foundations. He permitted Apollos, who was not an assistant, to work in Corinth (I Cor. 3:6). But none of these came like the intruders seeking to correct the Gospel Paul had preached (cf. 11:4). When the intruders acted like this, they were in fact destroying the foundations Paul had laid.

We all have areas for which we feel ourselves pastorally responsible as ministers or priests, as parents or teachers. We do not like those who come and, whether in fact or by implication, correct what we are doing. We regard them as intruders. There are, however, few pioneer areas left where like Paul we can claim to have laid the foundations; perhaps parenthood is the sole one. But once we have been given responsibility for an area, we soon begin to look on it as our own. What minister has not been troubled by people with odd views coming along to disturb *his* or *her* flock! What parents have not been the recipients of good advice on how to rear their children or have not experienced others teaching them how to think and behave in ways which they themselves consider wrong, for example, permissiveness in morality or a wrong-headed attitude to the Bible! Dare we repulse such people with the confidence of a Paul? If so, we must see that like him our confidence does not arise out of ourselves but comes from God. We also need to be certain that we do not get hot under the collar for the wrong reasons, for example, because the area is *ours*. When years afterwards we look back on such incidents, we often see that what we once thought was an intrusion actually worked for the good of those for whom we were responsible.

This passage should perhaps also point us in quite another direction. We react strongly when others enter the area of our concern. Do we take care to see we do not enter their areas? Do others say of us what, in effect, Paul said of his intruders, "Who do they think they are, interfering in our affairs?" We see something that is wrong and believe we can put it right. Do we stop long enough to consider whether we ought to interfere and whether if we do we have the capability of putting right what is wrong? It is not enough to compare ourselves with others (v. 12) and act as they do. We need to be continually thinking through the area of our legitimate responsibility.

II Corinthians 11:1–6
Paul's Jealousy for the Corinthians

So far Paul has dealt gently with his opponents. This changes as we move from generalities to specific issues. We can say this though we cannot fully identify these issues. His original readers will have had no trouble in doing so.

In order to deal with his opponents, Paul will need to talk a lot about himself because of what they have said about him and his teaching. It is always difficult to talk about oneself without seeming to brag (see "Playing the Fool"), and Paul is aware that what he will say is going to sound like bragging. He has already done a little (10:13) and rebuked his opponents for doing it (10:12,18). He begins by acknowledging that it is foolish

100

(the word runs through this passage, cf. 11:16–19; 12:6,11) to boast or commend oneself. It is foolish because those who do so will sooner or later be found out, even if only in minor inexactitudes. Yet Paul has to take the risk because of the activity of his opponents.

He boasts first of his love for the Corinthians who are his converts, longing that they continue in the faith so that when Christ returns he may present them to him as a father would present his virgin daughter to her husband. Yet he fears that they may be led astray by the intruders as Eve was by the serpent. These intruders came preaching and teaching another Jesus than the one Paul had preached, offering a Spirit different from the Spirit Paul had offered, and proclaiming a gospel other than Paul's true gospel. Will his converts respect his loving care or accept those who oppose him? The latter may claim to be the only legitimate apostles, but Paul is also a legitimate apostle having as good a right to be heard as they. He is confident he can convince them if given a fair hearing, even allowing that he may not be the world's greatest orator, for he is not deficient in that true knowledge, which is the knowledge of God.

That summarizes what Paul says in these verses, but a number of puzzling features need further examination.

Sexual language is often used in religion to explicate the intimate relationship of worshipers and deity because it describes one of the closest relationships that can exist among human beings. In the Old Testament it is used of the relation of Israel (wife) to God (husband); see Hosea chapters 1—3; Ezekiel chapters 16 and 23; Isaiah 50:1 and 54:1–6; Psalm 45; Song of Solomon. And in the New Testament see Mark 2:18–20; John 3:29–30; Romans 7:4; Ephesians 5:22–33; Revelation 19: 1–10; 21:1–9; 22:17. It has continued to be used ever since in Christian thought, especially during the Middle Ages. Since it is a metaphor, it can be adapted to suit varying purposes, and Paul has adapted it here to his immediate needs. The bridegroom, as here, is usually Christ, but unusually here, the bride is the local church and not the whole church (it is never the individual in the New Testament). The local church is of course the manifestation of the whole church in a particular area.

Paul allots himself an unexpected position in relation to the marriage as either its broker (the one who brings the parties together and arranges the terms of the dowry) or more probably as the bride's father. The parties were betrothed when Paul

101

first preached in Corinth, but the marriage has not yet taken place. Until it does, it is Paul's duty to protect the bride so that he may deliver her as a virgin to Christ. Fearful he may not succeed, he talks of "jealousy." Normally we would speak of the future husband or wife as "jealous" but not of the father or the marriage broker. Jealousy, says Denney, is "love tormented by fear" (p. 313). Paul loves the bride but is haunted by the fear that she may be seduced by the intruders from "her one husband," Christ, and be married to "another Jesus." Clearly the seduction, likened to that of Eve in Eden, has not yet been fully accomplished, and Paul still hopes to win back the "devotion" of the bride to Christ.

When Paul speaks of "devotion" he does not mean that he is worried that the Corinthians may not pray enough but that their "thoughts," that is, their understanding of Christ, may be led astray. (Two adjectives are joined to "devotion"; some translations have only one; the Greek manuscripts sometimes have one, sometimes the other, and often both; the meaning is not affected.) So he directs all his energies to seeing that the church remains faithful to Christ. As the founder of the church in Corinth, Paul wishes to present it to Christ when he returns to earth. Only then will the marriage be consummated. (Marriage and the parousia are linked also at Matt. 22:1–14; 25:1–13; Luke 12:35–40; Rev. 19:1–10.) In common with believers of his time Paul thought the parousia would not be long delayed. It is not possible for us to think in the same way as Paul about presenting Christians to Christ. We may labor to preserve those for whom we have a pastoral responsibility so that they are not led astray, but we know that before the end comes there will be many others, as faithful as ourselves, who will also labor over them.

If we wish to discover what Paul thought his opponents were teaching, verse 4 is the key, but unlike the original readers, it is difficult for us to turn it and unlock the meaning. With the phrase, "for if some one," Paul is not bringing forward a hypothetical case, as some older translations imply, but referring to the actual state of affairs in Corinth and describing either what the intruding group or its ringleader has been saying. Note that Paul does not accuse his rivals of introducing another or non-Christian God but another Jesus, a Spirit (this should probably be spelled with a capital "S" as indicating the Spirit of God) and a gospel other than those which he had originally preached in Corinth. Paul is alarmed that his rivals use the same terms as he does, for they then sound as Christian as he himself is. There are still those who come into established congregations and use Christian language but whose basic position is far from the true Christian position. They often deceive those who lack theological understanding. It is possible his rivals preached a theology of works (see Romans and Galatians for Paul's refutation of such a theology), but there are other false views. Some proclaimed a salvation through knowledge as opposed to a salvation through a suffering Christ, with that knowledge coming through initiation into secrets (additional revelations?) or philosophical reflection. Others stressed the importance of experiences of an emotional nature, for example, speaking with tongues, without regard to moral behavior (see I John for the contrast, e.g., 2:4–11).

Those who exercise pastoral responsibility need to recognize and attack non-Christianity or partial Christianity when it presents itself in Christian form. Yet they need to be careful in doing this, for down through the church's history, people have shown themselves to be adept at denouncing views which have later been accepted as orthodox (consider how John Wesley was rejected). Sometimes narrow definitions of Christianity have been drawn up and everyone forced to toe the line or to be branded as an enemy. Tolerance is therefore necessary. Before we jump in too readily to criticize other Christians, we need to recognize that the New Testament contains a much greater variety of ways in which the Christian faith is expressed than those who draw up narrow definitions often allow. Christianity cannot be defined only in terms of faith over against works or only as visiting orphans and widows in their affliction and keeping oneself unstained from the world (James 1:27). We can understand and accept the diversity of view within the New Testament once we realize that each view arises out of a particular situation and its need.

Paul asks the Corinthians to treat him at least as equal with his rivals, the "superlative apostles." Who are these? We normally think of the apostles as the Twelve whom Jesus chose, with Paul added as an extra. The word "apostle" however is used in the New Testament in a variety of ways. Basically it indicates people who are sent, and so Paul uses it in 8:23 (i.e., messengers) of those he sent to Corinth (cf. Phil. 2:29). In Romans 16:7 he terms Andronicus and Junia apostles, though these were certainly not among the Twelve. If then Paul's opponents called themselves apostles, this does not mean that they were members of the Twelve (Paul would hardly have described them the way he does in vv. 13–15 if that had been so). All the term implies is that they had been sent by some person (e.g., James the brother of Jesus) or by some body of people (e.g., the leaders of the church in Jerusalem) or by Christ. That they termed themselves "apostles of Christ" suggests that they claimed the last. If so, both Paul and his rivals made the same claim.

One accusation they made against Paul must have rankled, for he refers to it now for the second time: He was unskilled in speaking (cf. 10:10). The art of speaking in public formed an important part of higher education in Greece and Rome. Paul, brought up in Tarsus and trained as a rabbi in Jerusalem, cannot have been totally ignorant of the art. But his letters show that he was not always careful to pursue an argument with purely logical precision. He often dealt with matters which in the light of his larger concerns seemed like side issues. So there is a kind of unrestrained excitedness about his writing. The same must have been true of his speaking, and the accusation will then have had some truth. Paul does not deny it but counters by saying that he is not unskilled in knowledge. By this he does not mean intellectual sophistication but knowledge of God. The one who knows God is able to do more than simply argue logically or theoretically about him. There is a personal element, a living and warm fellowship, in knowing God just as there is in the way we know our friends. It is this knowledge of God that Paul claims and by implication denies to his opponents.

We have now covered the difficult details of this passage. It is important to return and read the summary of its argument, which we gave in our third paragraph, so that the details fall into place and we realize again the depth of Paul's care for his converts.

II Corinthians 11:7–11
Paul Never a Financial Burden

The subject changes abruptly as Paul turns to meet a fresh accusation: about his financial support. It is not a new charge. He had written about it earlier (I Cor. 9:3–18) when he allowed that apostles had the right to maintenance though he had not availed himself of it. He claimed then that his refusal did not make him any less an apostle than Peter. His refusal was deliberate. As a Jew, Paul, like every good Jew, and especially a good rabbi, had learned a trade from which he could support himself. This trade was probably some kind of work with leather or skins for which Tarsus was a center. When he went out as a missionary he had maintained himself from the start by plying his trade (I Thess. 2:9; II Thess. 3:8). He had done this in Corinth (cf. Acts 18:3; I Cor. 4:12; 9:6). However, at some stage of his mission in Corinth, he had accepted money from the Christians in Macedonia (v. 9). Probably he was willing to accept support from churches after he had left them; it freed him to evangelize. But when he first went to a new city he worked for his living, so that he could maintain his independence and be under no obligation to those who were in their early days as Christians. There was probably another reason. He did not wish to be classed with the many traveling philosophers and teachers who accepted money for their instruction and sometimes exacted quite high fees. Some of them were not over scrupulous in the value they gave for those fees.

We have been reading between the lines here, for Paul does not say precisely why he refused financial support. He does, however, justify himself by saying that, in making no claim on the generosity of the Corinthians, he had abased himself. In doing so he was imitating the behavior of his Lord at its deepest level (8:9; Phil. 2:5–11). It would also be a fulfillment of what he said in 4:12, "death is at work in us, but life in you." By his action the Corinthians are exalted, and Paul again demonstrates his love for them.

If we are engaged in paid Christian work, does Paul expect

105

us to follow him in refusing any form of payment? He is not laying down here a rule for all Christians. In I Corinthians 9:14 he accepts the saying of the Lord that "those who proclaim the gospel should get their living" from it. This should be the normal practice though there are occasions for following Paul's example. When missionaries first went to the third world social and economic conditions were so different from what they had left that they could hardly have found suitable work. It was necessary to accept support from the home base. (When Paul moved to a new Greek city the conditions were almost the same as those in which he had been brought up at Tarsus.) Yet if we grant that, it must also be said that there is perhaps too great a dissociation today between the full-time paid workers of the church and the life of the world. In some areas the church has benefited from those (e.g., worker-priests) who have refused deliberately to accept money and have worked to support themselves. This is not a new thing. In past times in many parts of rural Europe, the minister was not given a salary but land to farm in order to maintain himself and his family.

The paid church worker can sometimes lose touch with the fears, anxieties, and problems of ordinary people. Those who think they never do so should recollect how often they themselves criticize denominational officials for losing touch with the real world and politicians and administrators for not understanding how most people actually live. That however is not all that has to be said. Good pastors regularly accept the insights of their congregations and are able in that way to enter genuinely and deeply into the fears and anxieties of their fellows. Money and time has been spent on their theological education, and it would be wasted if they had to spend a large part of their time earning a living in some secular occupation.

This is not all Paul has to say on financial support and he returns to it in 12:14–18 (see notes there).

II Corinthians 11:12–15
The Deceitfulness of False Apostles

It was not immediately clear from verses 7–11 why Paul brought up the question of financial support. It now becomes clearer. His opponents have been claiming that they worked on the same principles as he did (v. 12; the Greek of this verse is difficult, indeed so difficult that some commentators have pointed out that it demonstrates Paul's admission in v. 6 that he was unskilled in speaking; the translation of the RSV and our explanation appear the most satisfactory). This claim could not be true since they accepted money. Paul has discovered a real chink in his opponents' armor, and he now exploits this to the full.

There is no other passage in his letters where he heaps on his opponents so much abuse in so few words. Unfortunately what he says tells us very little about his real objections to them. Accepting money was itself no sin (see on vv. 7–11), nor would it stultify any claim to be an apostle, for Peter had done so (I Cor. 9:3–7). But were his opponents genuine apostles (for the use of the word see vv. 1–6)? They claimed to be apostles of Christ. Did this mean they had gone about on earth with Jesus, seen the risen Lord, and were as well qualified to be one of the Twelve as Matthias (Acts 1:21–22)? Or had they claimed like Paul that the risen Lord appeared to them (more than five hundred Christians had seen him, I Cor. 15:6) and called them to be apostles? Either assertion would have been difficult to disprove, and Paul wastes no time vetting their pedigree. His rejection of them rests on what they say and do. As supposed workmen for God they are deceivers. They are neither true emissaries of Christ nor are they really engaged in the service of the Lord.

In reality they are not Christ's servants but Satan's. Satan passes himself off as someone who is good; what else can one expect from his servants? As master, so servant! Paul draws here on Jewish legends which described Satan as disguising himself in order to deceive. He seduced Eve, and if he did so, it will have been by charming her rather than by terrifying her. Now he is said to pass himself off as an angel of light. In biblical imagery evil is depicted as dark and the true nature of Satan as darkness (Col. 1:13). But Satan is at war with humanity and one stratagem in war is to wear the enemy's uniform; in that way his lines can be penetrated and destroyed from within. More danger has always lain for the church in inner corruption than in outer persecution. Paul fears his rivals have so presented themselves as genuine servants of God that his converts will be led astray. His rivals' success, however, cannot last for ever. Soon they will have to answer for their deeds when, like everyone else, they appear before the judgment seat of Christ (5:10). The result will be their condemnation.

The kind of language Paul uses here of his opponents seems extreme, yet it has figured repeatedly in Christian and non-Christian controversy through the centuries. Indeed it has often been much more abusive in later periods. In the New Testament itself Judas is said to be possessed by Satan (Luke 22:3; John 13:27); the devil is the father of the Jews who oppose Jesus (John 8:44); heretics are antichrists (I John 2:18; cf. also Rev. 2:9; 3:9). Can the use of such language here and in later Christian times be justified? Certainly not always, for those who have been so described have often turned out later to be accepted as orthodox. Is Paul's unusually sharp invective acceptable in the present instance? He has been venomously attacked, and his converts are in danger of being seduced. He cannot stand aside indifferently. But to be able to answer our question fully, we would need more information than Paul has given us about his opponents and their teaching. What he writes he writes as a warning to the Corinthians. It is not about them that he uses his strong language but about those who have been disturbing them. He does not even say it directly to his rivals but writes it. Would he have said all of it if he had met them face to face? His critics accused him of frightening people with his letters but being much less forthright in personal encounter (10:9-10). There may have been some truth in that charge. Face to face with his opponents, he may have moderated his language because he saw them as those for whom Christ died. They became men and women to be won, no longer rivals to be condemned.

What of ourselves? It is easy to condemn people when absent, but when we meet them as living people, as those for whom we need to care, do some of our criticisms die on our lips?

Our tone changes not because we are too embarrassed or afraid to say what we think but because what we think changes. It is important that we take great care when we denounce others. Our words can too easily run away with us. The denunciatory words of Scripture have been regularly appropriated by Christian controversialists and thrown at those they disliked. If we do this, let us remember that our end will correspond with our deeds (v. 15) and that whoever causes one of these little ones who believe in Jesus to sin it would be better for him if a great mill-stone were hung around his neck and he were thrown into the sea (Mark 9:42). The heretic may be won back from his ways more often and more permanently by love than by invective. Above all it is important to be sure first that the heretic is a heretic and not an erring child of Christ and, secondly, that it is not we ourselves in our self-confidence and arrogance who are the erring children.

II Corinthians 11:16—12:13
Self-commendation

The denunciation of opponents is easy, and too many Christians indulge in it. To be genuinely effective it needs to be supported with substantial arguments and these Paul now supplies. His opponents have made claims about their position, abilities, and importance. His own claims are in every respect equal to theirs if not superior. He first justifies his need to boast about himself (11:16–21*a*) and then does so in three different areas: his general mission activity (11:21*b*–29), one particular humiliating experience (11:30–33), a vision and the lesson he learned from it (12:1–10). He ends by asking forgiveness for boasting (12:11–13).

The Need to Boast (11:16–21*a*)

Paul is hesitant to boast because he knows the only valid boast for any Christian is a boast about Christ (see 10:17f.). Yet to show that his claims are as good as those of his rivals, he must now do what he has already condemned in them and boast about himself. Boasting is "foolishness" (see 11:1); only fools

109

brag about themselves. All sensible people, even non-Christians, would agree with Paul that it is wrong to blow one's own trumpet, though they might offer other reasons (e.g., "pride comes before a fall"). Foolish though it may be, Paul will do it if it is the only way he can discomfit the intruders. He writes here, then, with deep irony (see especially v. 19). He does not want the Corinthians to accept him as a fool but as an apostle. But if playing the fool will bring them more quickly to that conclusion, he will play the fool.

Since boasting about oneself is not a proper Christian activity, it is not possible to boast about spiritual matters but only about "worldly" (v. 18; for the word see 1:17 and 10:2). It may not seem to us, as we read on, that Paul boasts only about worldly things; his account of his rapture seems an exception; being beaten with rods is not what we normally think of as "worldly." It is then not so much the things themselves that are worldly as the spirit in which they are offered. What motivated his opponents in their boasts was not love of Christ but their own self-importance. Such boasting is "worldly," no matter what its content, and those who do it are fools.

Paul, of course, is not so much worried by the nature of the boasts the intruders make as he is that the Corinthians may be taken in by those boasts and desert the true gospel. They imagine they are wise in deciding in favor of Paul's rivals because of what his rivals have said about themselves. They ought however to be wise enough to recognize that Paul's own boasting has a more substantial basis.

The way the Corinthians "bear" his rivals must appear to us as most surprising. They not merely listen to and accept their boasts but allow them to trample on them and their rights (v. 20). Like slaves the Corinthians are forced to provide for their maintenance beyond anything that is reasonable ("prey upon you"; "they eat you out of house and home" as we might say). The false apostles even use physical violence against them. Of course those were rougher days, and many of the Corinthians were slaves and accustomed to violence. Paul, however, had never treated them in any of these ways. With that they could not disagree for they themselves had accused him of being too soft (10:1,10). Perhaps the real fools in this situation were not Paul and his rivals who boasted but the poor duped Corinthians!

Violence is no longer acceptable as a way of exercising pastoral care, and we would think it equally wrong to take any

110

kind of unfair advantage over those for whom we are pastorally responsible. Yet, regrettably, there are still those who play on the piety of their followers in such a way as to preserve themselves in wealth and ease.

Paul had a deeper doubt about his boasting than we have mentioned up to now. It emerges in the seeming parenthesis of verse 17. In boasting Paul has not been gentle and meek like his Lord, nor can he claim his Lord's authority for what he has done. Has he then been deliberately behaving in an unchristian manner? We face here a basic dilemma: A good end is sought, but the only means to attain it are tainted. Superficially Paul appears worried that he may seem like a fool in boasting, but deep down he is more worried that he may not have the Lord's authority. He is clearer than most people about what carries the Lord's authority, yet he remembers the needs of his church and seemingly goes against what the Lord would appear to authorize. Or does he really err in that way? There is no absolute will of God which lays down authoritative laws holding in every situation, except, of course, the two great commandments of love. What God desires is always a particular form of conduct in a particular situation. Paul provides this by his boasting. Yet he has a feeling that something may be wrong. His conscience is sensitive both to God and to his converts. If a choice has to be made, his converts win out! Are we all as sensitive as Paul? We do something which others see as transgressing God's will, and we respond by saying that we did it because of the need of others. Have we been as conscious in our action as Paul was in his that we may have transgressed the Lord's authority?

Paul Boasts About His Work (11:21*b*–29)

Paul's rivals have boasted; now he will boast. If there is to be a contest in who can brag the most, he is sure that he will come out on top. Not that he is happy about it ("I am speaking as a fool"), but what else can he do? We do not know the boasts and criticisms his rivals have made and can only guess what they may have been from his reply.

They cannot simply have denied that he was a Jew; they must have said he was not as good or as real a Jew as themselves. Probably they said that they were Hebrew (or Aramaic) speaking Jews who were not descended from proselytes and could trace their ancestry physically as well as theologically (Gal. 3:29) back to Abraham the first Jew. As Israelites they belonged to

111

God's chosen people. They may also have implied thereby a special relation to Jesus, for example, that they had actually known him in Palestine, a relation which a person like Paul who had been brought up in Tarsus could not have had. If indeed they made such a claim, Paul had no real reply. But like any wise controversialist, he does not expose the weak side of his case. Instead he proceeds at once to its strongest—his actual service of Christ.

In verse 22 he only claims equality with his rivals; now in verse 23 he claims much more ("I am a better one," note his use of comparatives). These rivals must have said they were servants of Christ. That Paul has already called them "servants of Satan" (vv. 14–15) does not mean he cannot now use the term they use of themselves. That kind of switch takes place regularly in controversy. Even at their own valuation of themselves Paul will show they fall far below him.

There is another difference between Paul's boasting in verse 22 and that in verses 23–29. In verse 22 he boasts about what he is by birth, but he had no voice in the choice of his parents. From verse 23 on he boasts about things over which he himself had control. So he now lists what has happened to him. Such lists or catalogues were then common. Roman emperors and oriental despots set up inscriptions listing their achievements. Paul can write as impressive and as long a list as any of them, but it is not one of successes but of sufferings. If his opponents have boasted of what they suffered and accomplished, Paul can outdo them.

Verse 23b is phrased in general terms. Apart from the reference to imprisonments, the remainder is detailed in what follows. No easy pattern can be forced on the list. It moves with a certain rhythm as do other passages in Paul (e.g., Rom. 8: 31–39; I Cor. 13). What he says falls broadly into three areas: (1) sufferings at the hands of others; (2) loss of the ordinary necessities of life, for example, food, clothing, sleep, which could come through the action of others but also from the sheer difficulty of travel in those days; (3) inward stress from worry about his churches.

The list is impressive as it stands and loses its effect if broken up and discussed in detail, yet a few items must be individualized. We do not know how many times or where Paul had been in prison prior to his writing of this portion of Second Corinthians. He may have been in prison in Ephesus (see I Cor.

112

15:32). He was in prison when he wrote to the Philippians (1:13) and to Philemon (v. 1), but these imprisonments were almost certainly later. Acts records only one imprisonment up to this time (16:23), no instances of the Jewish punishment of forty lashes less one, and only one occasion on which Paul was beaten with rods (16:22–23; something which as a Roman citizen he could have expected to escape; cf. 22:25–29). Acts 14:19 records the one instance of stoning but no shipwreck prior to the writing of this letter. One of these must have been severe for Paul survived, probably floating on bits of wreckage, for twenty-four hours before either reaching land or being picked up. If Acts amazes us with what Paul endured, then this list shows how inadequate its account really is and how much more Paul suffered than we can ever know.

Travelers endured many perils, swollen rivers, brigands, lack of food and water, excessive heat and cold. Even when Paul was settled for a period in a city, his tribulations did not cease. If he refused help from the local church, he might be without food for a time or have to work long into the night to support himself. In the cities he also always ran the peril of mob violence, perhaps incited by Jews (e.g., Acts 13:50; 14:19; 17:5).

Surprisingly the list of dangers refers to perils from other Christians (v. 26) whom Paul terms "false brethren." Who are these? Perhaps Judaizers who regarded his preaching to Gentiles and admission of them to the church as contrary to God's will (Acts 15:1–2; Gal. 2:4) or those rivals who were even now destroying his work in Corinth (cf. vv. 13–15).

Paul's final point about his service to Christ relates to the inward wear and tear on his mind and soul, something even more difficult to bear than his physical sufferings. There were sleepless nights arising from his anxiety about one or another of his churches. There is evidence of this pressure in our letter. Worry about Corinth led him to leave off evangelization in Troas (2:12–13). After sending the intermediate or painful letter, he was for a while torn by regret (7:8). The language he uses about his opponents (11:12–15) indicates how much he must have been worried by what was happening in Corinth. And Corinth was not the only church about which he would be worried. Each church that he had founded had its own particular concerns which were being continually reported to him, which he could only deal with by letter, and for news of which he would anxiously wait. One of his converts is lost through the

113

words or actions of another or through persecution, and Paul is indignant (a stronger translation, "burn with indignation," is justified). His indignation must often have been increased by his sheer inability to do anything. Distances were great, travel was slow; by the time he learned of trouble it might be too late to do anything about it. All this would bear harshly on him.

In the light of that, what does Paul mean by "Who is weak, and I am not weak?" We expect him to say he would be strong where others are weak in order to help them overcome their weakness. But what he says is another case of the transference of qualities which we encountered in 1:3–7 and 4:12. Converts are weak; Paul's strength flows into them. They become strong; Paul becomes weak. Paul's weakness is the same weakness as that of the crucified Christ: from it flows strength.

It is an amazing picture of Paul that emerges. How little we really know about him! How many untold stories of courage, compassion, and endurance lie behind this list! And it all must have taken place in the space of a mere dozen years! The picture moreover displays only the externals of his life. There is nothing about his understanding and expression of his faith which to us is perhaps his more permanent memorial.

We need to be cautious here and neither claim too much nor make the wrong claims. There have been others who have endured as much in the cause of patriotism or political belief (e.g., marxists under right-wing dictatorships, humanists in communist countries) or for their faith in another religion (e.g., members of the Baha'i faith in Iran). We can do nothing other than admire them, whoever they are, when they endure as Paul did. In his case we can see how extreme suffering, even at the hands of others, left no bitterness or hardness. The suffering is part of his attempt to be like Christ. All his letters reflect his joy in serving his Lord (in this letter see 6:10). They also show how he remembered his converts in prayer. It is to him we owe the hymn of love in First Corinthians, chapter 13. His greatness only truly appears when we set these things alongside both the power of his mind and the extent of his sufferings.

There is no lesson which we can draw for ourselves or others from this passage other than to wonder again at what Paul was and at what he endured for the gospel. We only tarnish his image if we start to compare ourselves with him—our lives

114

are so different, our afflictions so minor. Let us pray that in them we may be found of like spirit with him.

A Humiliating Experience (11:30–33)

Paul has just referred to his weakness (v. 29). He stops to comment that his boasting is not about things which display his importance and significance but about those in which that weakness appears. He has taken this line because he has not wanted to boast ("must"). Only a "fool," a fool for Christ's sake (I Cor. 4:10), would boast in the kind of things in which Paul boasts. He could have been a leading rabbi in Jerusalem, and that without a financial care in the world, for he may well have come from a wealthy family. Who then can doubt his sincerity? In case there should be any doubt he summons God as his witness, and the brief doxology lends solemnity to what he has said (cf. Rom. 1:25; 9:5).

With this renewed reference to the purpose and content of his boasting, the rhythm of the passage is lost, and when he begins again we seem to move from poetry to prose as he recounts in detail one moment in which his life was at risk. The direct and simple manner in which he tells the story lends no support to the idea that he is repudiating some slander of his opponents, for example, that from the beginning he had run away from trouble like a coward or that his escape in a basket made him a figure of ridicule. It is rather a clear and indisputable example of his weakness. It may have stuck in his mind as outstanding simply because it happened at the beginning of his ministry, the first "undignified" incident in which he had been involved.

The story itself seems to be the same as that recorded in Acts 9:23–25, though there are differences of detail. Luke was dependent on the tradition handed down, probably in the church in Damascus. Paul was writing much nearer the event and had been involved in it, so his account will represent more correctly what happened. Even as it stands it presents us with some historical difficulties which the academic commentaries explore. Presumably Paul preached in Damascus and disturbed public order in some way or other by what he said in the Jewish synagogues. Aretas or his representative took action, probably because of Jewish complaints as we see happening so often later in Acts.

Paul Is Taught to Depend on God (12:1–10)

Reluctantly Paul continues the boasting into which he has been forced by the Corinthians. (The translations of v. 1 differ because of an uncertainty about the Greek text, but there is no uncertainty about the main thrust of Paul's argument.) He moves now to a new area of his life, and such an unusual one that we must assume the Corinthians had themselves introduced it. Either they expected good leaders to have had "visions and revelations" (the two words mean much the same in our context), or Paul's rivals laid claim to them. Such experiences were viewed in the ancient world in many religions as a special sign of God's favor. Had Paul been so marked out by God?

He had been—at least once. The way he refers to the experience as taking place fourteen years earlier suggests that he did not have such experiences regularly. This one had been of so personal a nature that he had kept it to himself all those years, for unless a spiritual experience would be helpful in building up a church there was no need to talk about it. In any case God had not allowed him to talk about its content ("things that cannot be told," v. 4). Since this section of Paul's letter was written probably around A.D. 56–58, the event itself (A.D. 42–45) took place during a period about which we know nothing of Paul's life. We cannot then relate it to any particular event therein.

Elsewhere he tells us about some of his other spiritual experiences: his conversion (Gal. 1:11–16; I Cor. 9:1; 15:8) and the revelation that led him to go to Jerusalem to defend the admission of Gentiles into the church (Gal. 2:2). Acts recounts similar experiences (16:9; 18:9; 22:17–21; 27:23). Since all these related directly to the advance of the gospel it was possible, indeed imperative, to communicate their essential message.

The present experience was of a very personal nature. The phrase "things (literally 'words') that cannot be told," is strange. Words by their very nature are to be told. What happened here was not then "beyond words" as if it was too wonderful for mere words to describe. Paul, rather, was not permitted to pass on what he had heard. He was given no message to communicate. This, of course, has not prevented speculation about it and from an early period writings were produced using his name and giving details of what he saw and heard.

The terms he uses suggest that his experience belonged

116

more to the ear than to the eye. In particular what he had was not just a vision of the Lord ("of the Lord," v. 1 refers to the source of his experience and not to its content) as he had had at his conversion. A repetition of that would not have been exceptional. There was also one essential difference from his conversion. Then Christ came down to him; here he is taken up, raptured, to Christ. The way he stresses that he was "caught up" shows that he viewed himself as passive during the experience. God had caught him up. He had not then induced the experience in himself by prayer, fasting, ascetic practice, or through the use of drugs. It was not something he could renew at will but an exceptional event, and nothing suggests that he expected other Christians to have similar experiences, not even church officials as a condition of their appointment!

Paul was given his vision and revelation in the third heaven and Paradise. "Heaven" is by no means a simple concept in Scripture. Sometimes it is depicted as God's dwelling place, while at others it is assumed that he lives beyond the heavens (in Heb. 4:14 Jesus passes through them to reach God). Evil powers are said to dwell in heaven (Eph. 6:12). The Jews believed in a plurality of heavens, usually seven in number but sometimes three as here. The third heaven is then the highest heaven reached by passing through the other two. It can equally be described as "Paradise," which some Jewish apocalyptic writings place in the "third heaven." Paradise often indicated for the Jews the place of the righteous dead. Perhaps then what Paul saw and was told about was the place of the afterlife rather than that he was given a preview of future events and the parousia.

Paul did not seek the experience and is forbidden to tell what he saw and heard. He is also unable to tell how it took place. He does not know whether his physical body was caught up with him or whether only some spiritual part of him went away by itself to Paradise. Judaism and the ancient world knew of both kinds of experience. All we can deduce is that when Paul had the experience he was alone, otherwise anyone who had been with him would have been able to tell him whether his body left earth or not!

At first sight when we read this passage, the experience seems to belong to someone other ("I know a man") than Paul. 117 However, the whole course of his argument depends on the fact that he has no one other than himself in mind; it would have been quite irrelevant to introduce another person. Why then does he speak as if the experience had happened to someone else? It is not as if he thought of himself as a split personality with an *alter ego,* which could go off on spiritual voyages of its own. Probably it arises out of his unwillingness even to appear to boast for self-advantage. It is proper to boast about others, never about oneself. Yet he has to introduce the experience in some way so that his rivals may not be the only ones to claim to have had visions and the like. Moreover if Paul was passive in the experience, he has no reason to boast. God chose that he should have it. So God should have all the glory (cf. 10:17).

The true follower of Jesus, the "man in Christ," should not be making claims about extraordinary spiritual experiences but about "weakness" (v. 5). But before Paul picks up again the theme of "weakness," he has one final remark to make about his experience: It was true (v. 6). At least if people brag about what has happened to them, let them brag about things that are true and not about what they have imagined. Paul does not provide any proof that it was true. In the nature of the case that would have been impossible, but such proof was not then so necessary as it might appear to be to our scientific minds, for people of that time did not regard such experiences as unusual.

Paul does not wish to linger on or to overstress his experience because the cross rather than any personal experience was always the subject of his preaching. All the suffering and weakness of which he boasted (11:23–29) have been in keeping with that cross. So also was the "thorn in the flesh," the "messenger of Satan," which he now introduces as another witness to his weakness.

No one knows with any certainty to what Paul refers by these two phrases. There was nothing to forbid him telling the Corinthians; presumably they already knew. We do not. The academic commentaries list and discuss the possibilities. The "thorn" clearly refers to something painful; even a thorn in a sensitive place, as under a fingernail, can be extremely painful. Paul's use here of "flesh" suggests to many commentators that he had in mind a bodily ailment, epilepsy, migraine, a speech impediment, ophthalmia, malaria. Others think the complaint may not have been physical but mental (e.g., bouts of depression or despair) or spiritual (e.g., some particular temptation), since for Paul the term "flesh" was not restricted to the physical sphere (cf. the list of works of the flesh in Gal. 5:19–21). Com-

118

mentators who concentrate on the phrase "messenger of Satan" tend to think of trouble coming to Paul from other people (e.g., persecutors, Christians who regarded him as a heretic). Whatever aggrieved him he clearly thinks of it as beginning at the time of his vision or as a consequence of it. It cannot then have been something to which he was always subject, for example, persecution or temptation. Equally it cannot have been a congenital physical illness or handicap, like a speech impediment, for that would always have been there. Some physical ailments also seem highly unlikely because no one who suffered from them could have accomplished Paul's missionary work or endured the sufferings listed in 11:23–29. Whatever or whoever it was, it continued with Paul at least up to the time of the writing of our letter (the "this" of v. 8 can equally be, probably ought to be, rendered "him" and the "it" rendered "he," both referring to "messenger"). He had prayed three times for its (his) removal. This would indicate its chronic nature if an illness, though it may have affected Paul only intermittently, or if an "enemy" his or her repeated attacks.

What does Paul mean when he also terms what assailed him a "messenger of Satan"? While both mental and physical illness were often believed in those days to be caused by Satan (Luke 13:16) that is not why Paul refers to Satan here. Whatever assailed him could have interfered with the preaching of the gospel. Satan seeks to hinder the gospel in every way possible, so the "thorn" can be described as "satanic." In actual fact Satan's plot came to nothing. Instead of slowing Paul down, the "thorn" worked to save him from spiritual pride and, therefore, served to advance the gospel. Note Paul's double reference in verse 7 to elation. He was "all up in the air" after his rapture to Paradise. He needed to be brought down to earth lest he give too great an importance to his rapture—and too little to the cross. The messenger of Satan saw to that.

When he first became aware of the thorn Paul did not see it in that light. So he prayed to God ("three times" need not be taken literally; it indicates that Paul prayed a number of times and that there came a time when he stopped praying) for the removal of what appeared to be humiliating him and interfering with his Christian service. Like all of us, Paul was not only ready to pray to God but also to tell him what the proper answer to the prayer should be! God answers prayer but not always in the way we expect, and not here in the way Paul expected.

119

However, when God did not take away the thorn, Paul realized its true purpose, and he was now also able to see his "rapture" in a truer perspective. There was nothing in it to boast about, for he had in no way earned it. God had given it, just as he had given the thorn.

The actual lesson he learned from God went much deeper. The Lord, that is, Jesus, said to him, "My grace is sufficient for you, for my power is made perfect in weakness." Paul does not tell us how Jesus said this to him. Perhaps a prophet spoke it in a service or he may have heard an inner voice or he may have just gradually become aware that this was God's message. In any case it was a revelation, and unlike that of verses 2–4, it was one which he could communicate to others. The experience might be personal, but the truth was one for all Christians.

We might have expected that Paul would have received an answer telling him to be content with things as they were: You have had your experience, now you have an affliction; you cannot always be on top of the world; you must take the rough with the smooth. Learn to live with your present situation and you will discover that every cloud has its silver lining. Equally Paul might have been told that suffering dignifies; borne patiently it strengthens character. It is true that that happens with some people, but there are also those whom suffering destroys because it embitters them. Paul again might have been told to depend on his own inner resources. He had been a Christian long enough for his character to be built up. If he looked into himself, he would find the strength to endure. Instead of any of these messages Paul received one that forced him to look not to himself but to God and God's power. Paul is not to fear his own weakness, for weakness belongs to the human condition, even to the saved human condition, and when accepted permits God's grace to operate

Grace often means the favor with which God looks at us and forgives us though we are undeserving. But, linked as here to power, it is also often used for the strength God gives by which Christians are enabled to live as Christians. It can only function where there is weakness and where that weakness is acknowledged. Sometimes when we attempt to teach others a new technique or skill (e.g., a grown-up with a child), we find they obstinately resist our instruction, thinking they know it all. It is then impossible to help them. But once they recognize their "weakness," we can come in with our "strength." So God cannot impart strength to us until we acknowledge our weakness. It was Paul's weakness in respect to the thorn in the flesh about which he could do nothing that led him to allow God in with his strength.

Once Paul had learned that the weakness which came from the messenger of Satan could be borne with God's strength, he learned something he could apply to all the weaknesses which afflicted him. So, very briefly, he sums up the long list of 11: 23–29 in the short list of verse 10. When he is weak and knows it then he can be strong, not with his own strength but with God's. The final words of verse 10 are a fitting climax to all that he has been saying about the various afflictions he has endured. They may get him down from time to time (if the thorn in the flesh had not done that he would never have prayed about it), but then he remembers that to carry on he should not be relying on his own inner reserves of strength but on God. He knows the heights of spiritual experience in vision and revelation; he knows the depths in the assaults of Satan's messenger. He lives between them by the grace of God. Superior to and more valuable than the vision of Paradise is the assurance, "My grace is sufficient for you, my power is made perfect in weakness."

A True Apostle (12:11–13)

Paul is coming to the end of his boasting, and he reiterates that he was forced into it by the Corinthians. It ought never to have been necessary. Since they were his converts, their very existence as Christians should have rendered self-praise unnecessary. Moreover they had seen the miracles he had performed among them and must have known many of the facts he gives in 11:22–29. But they had not stood up for him. Instead they had been silent and had accepted others as being superior to him. Who these others are is not clear. The Corinthians termed them apostles presumably because they gave themselves this title. Paul has already claimed equality with them in 11:5 (see also "Paul and His Opponents").

It appears Paul's rivals had called him a "nothing" or a "nobody." It is something he would gladly have said of himself, for by himself he was nothing; whatever he was, he was that by the grace of God (cf. I Cor. 15:9–10). It hurt him however when others said he was nothing, for they did not mean to imply by it that God had made him great! Yet whether others call him a "nobody" or not he is still by God's appointment a true apostle. That cannot be taken from him.

The dispute about Paul's apostleship began very soon after

121

the end of his original mission in Corinth, for he has already been compelled to substantiate his position in I Corinthians 9:1. He does so on the grounds that the risen Jesus appeared to him. Now, apparently, his opponents are offering other criticisms of his position. The true apostle is one who works miracles (the Twelve were sent out with power to heal and exorcise, Mark 3:15; 6:7,13) and who is maintained by the churches he founds. Paul easily met the first of these requirements (v. 12). Though we have no reports of him healing in Corinth there is no reason to doubt that he did so. Acts tells us what he did in other cities (e.g., 13:11; 14:10; 16:18). He himself alludes to his miracles in Romans 15:18–19 and in I Thessalonians 1:5. Note that Paul writes "were performed" and not "I performed." The passive voice is often used in Scripture to denote God as the real cause of what happens. Paul was both passive under God as God healed and also "patient." Though healing was exhausting he patiently endured and did not abandon the practice. We may observe that if Paul's thorn in the flesh was an illness, he was not healed from it.

Paul cannot meet the second objection to his apostleship so easily: He had not accepted maintenance. Yet was that something really to be held against him? Paul lapses into heavy sarcasm, "Forgive me this wrong!" It is difficult to know what other kind of answer he could have given. He had already explained his practice in I Corinthians 9:3–18. Yet sarcasm is never a good approach to others. It rarely heals breaches. That Paul resorts to it now shows how deep is the cleft between himself and the Corinthians.

Reading between the lines we sense Paul is replying to the Corinthians who have set up norms for determining who are true apostles, though it is not fully clear what the norms were. To us it probably seems strange that Paul should affirm his legitimacy by appealing to his miracles. We would count as more important his success in mission and his teaching and counseling of his churches. Yet Paul was not able to choose the criteria by which he was being judged. He probably did not even approve of them, yet what could he do but reply in their terms? The choice of criteria for the selection of those who are to exercise pastoral care is important (and this does not refer just to the pastor). We should not be satisfied with surface criteria (ability to raise money, attract large crowds, organize) but look into personal qualities of character. Equally we should not criticize on false norms those who are already exercising pastoral care.

Playing the Fool

We despise those who brag, yet in what we have been reading, Paul has done quite a lot of it. Earlier he had spoken of commending himself (3:1; 4:2; 5:12). Most of those who boast do not realize they are doing it. It is a sign of grace on Paul's part that he did realize and that he saw its foolishness. Since a comparison with others is inherent in boasting, it may involve belittling them. Since it is never far away from exaggeration, there is the continual danger of untruth.

Paul claims that when he boasts he speaks the truth (12:6). Does he do so? Many of his boasts were factual and could easily have been checked (e.g., his Jewish origin, the number of times he had been beaten), but no one saw his rapture to Paradise. The claim that he was a better servant of Christ than his rivals (11:23) was a value judgment by its very nature, and his rivals would have denied it, or they would never have been his rivals.

Paul excuses his boasting because he has been forced into it. But even then he may boast more than is necessary or about the wrong things. He says he puts limits on his boasting (10: 13,15), and many of the areas in which he refrains from boasting are those in which we would expect a braggart to boast (see below).

Positively he boasts about his Jewishness, what he suffered in the service of Christ, a thorn in the flesh given him by Satan. These show his weakness, though they also exhibit his sheer power of physical endurance. He only boasts about one spiritual experience (12:2–4); only by accident do we learn that he spoke in tongues (I Cor. 14:6), and surely he exercised the charismatic gifts of prophecy and healing, but he does not boast about them. He boasts that he did not accept upkeep from his converts. He boasts, though he does not use the word, that he converted them and betrothed them to Christ (11:2). Consequently he can boast of his position of authority over them (10:8) and of his display of the signs of an apostle among them.

Surprisingly he does not boast about the number of churches he founded, the number of converts he made, and the number of people he healed. He does not remind us of the depth of his training as a rabbi and his profound understanding

123

of Christian truth, nor does he draw us back repeatedly to his amazing conversion. While he tells us how much he suffered for Christ, he does not stress his sheer physical powers of endurance.

If Paul boasts, is it then legitimate for other Christians to do so? If we boast simply to build up our ego before others, that is clearly wrong. Yet at times, like Paul, we may be forced to boast to defend the gospel. The gospel can never be dissociated from its servants. To clear it of false accusation, they may need to clear themselves. But if we boast we need, like Paul, to recognize that it is foolishness. We should take no pleasure in it but rather be ashamed. We should also take care about what we boast and boast only of those things in which we are weak and the grace of God is strong—and yet, even here, there is the danger that we glorify ourselves by saying, "Look at *me;* God's grace is at work in *me!*" In all our boasting we should ever remember that eventually we have to account before the judgment seat of Christ (5:10) for every idle or deliberate word we speak about ourselves.

II Corinthians 12:14–21
A Third Visit to Corinth

Paul is about to visit Corinth for the third time. The first had been the original mission and the second the "painful" or "sorrowful" visit of 2:1. As he now plans to go again, he realizes that the problem of his maintenance will recur, so since he has no intention of changing this policy he again defends it (cf. 11:7–12). When writing letters we often return to subjects with which we have apparently finished when we see fresh angles that need further treatment.

As their original missioner he is their father and they his children (I Cor. 4:15; cf. Philem. 10). Parents normally do not look to their children for financial support. There are exceptions. Elderly parents may sign over property and other assets for tax purposes and then expect to be supported. That would not have happened in the ancient world. Families near the poverty line may look to their children to earn something, not to support the parents but simply to keep the family together. Paul then can expect his argument to be effective. It is true that children today often resent any suggestion of dependence on their parents; so what Paul says needs to be used carefully. Modern missionaries have been continually accused of adopting paternalistic attitudes towards their churches and of failing to hand over control to their members. Probably all who exercise pastoral care are tempted to treat those for whom they are responsible as children and not to recognize that they mature. Parents are particularly prone to this. So are politicians who withhold information because they think people are not mature enough to accept the truth. Doctors conceal from patients what they decide the patients are unable to bear.

Paul, for his part, probably thought he was sparing the Corinthians in not seeking maintenance. Did they feel themselves robbed of responsibility? People normally mature when they are allowed to shape their own lives. Paternalism stifles growth. Perhaps Paul did not realize that one of the better ways of creating a relationship with others is to seek their help as Jesus sought that of the woman at the well (John 4:7).

His refusal to receive financial support came in the end, however, from his passionate readiness to give his whole being for them ("spend and be spent"). If he has a private income, he will use it joyfully to help them and will go far beyond that in spending himself for them. "Your souls" here is just another way of saying "you." Paul is not thinking simply of their eternal salvation but of their whole existence. He is willing to give himself for whatever will contribute to their good—and this includes their material good, for he has saved them money in not accepting support. The long catalogue of sufferings in 11: 23–29 shows how he spent himself (cf. Phil. 2:17). He would allow death to work in him, so that life might work in them (4:12). How do his passionate declarations of love fit in with his refusal of support, his refusal to give them responsibility? People of that time would probably not have seen this as a question, for they lived in a less democratic age. It is a continual question for us. How can we affirm our deep love for others and yet refuse to give up control over them? Again parents are those who feel this dilemma most keenly, but all who exercise pastoral care need to be aware of the peril.

Paul loves them. He tries to love them more. Yet everything seems to be going wrong. Their love is not growing (v. 15

125

b). Forces are at work in Corinth, so that the more he tries to come to terms with his converts the less successful he appears to be. But Paul will not allow this to affect him or their lack of gratitude to quench his love for them. He will continue to show his love by refusing maintenance.

Money often complicates pastoral relationships. Paul may have thought that by refusing it he would make things easier. He would be free to say what he liked to the Corinthians. They however probably felt that when they did not pay him they had no control over him. In actual fact money had not been entirely eliminated. There was the collection for the poor in Jerusalem (see chapters 8,9). The suspicion got around that if Paul was refusing maintenance then it was because he was living off that money. His messengers were siphoning off some of it into his pocket (vv. 17–18). Paul mentions Titus because Titus stood so near him that if anybody was involved it must be he. This seems the most likely understanding of these rather obscure verses. Yet if there are suspicions, Paul seems confident that they will not come to anything and that both he and Titus will be seen to have acted with the same honesty (v. 18).

He has been talking so much about himself all through these last chapters that he realizes the wrong impression may have been created. He is not coming to Corinth to make excuses for himself but to deal with the trouble there. If excuses are in order, he will make them to God who is his judge and not to the Corinthians. Indeed if there is to be any judging done in Corinth, he will do it himself. But judging will be secondary to his main purpose—to build up his converts in the faith. All he is doing now is getting out of the way some doubts and suspicions on their part, which might prevent him from doing precisely that.

Paul knows what he would like to find when he arrives in Corinth: an undivided church eager to bring to the rest of Corinth the gospel of reconciliation which had served to heal its own divisions. He fears that instead he will find a church rent by internal dissension with many factions, only some of them supporting him or perhaps even entirely united against him in rejecting both his divine authority and his gospel. He lists eight sins, all of which surface when there are disagreements. If he finds them lost in self-opinionated squabbling, which is not what he wishes, then they may find him not what they wish. Unable to build up, he will have to tear down (13:10; cf. 10:8).

126

Yet Paul may not have to rebuke only those who have slid into excessive partisanship. There are also some who have been guilty of sexual sins ("impurity, immorality, licentiousness" can refer to nothing else) and have shown no signs of repentance. The last few chapters may have had no references to such sins, but they were present in Corinth from the beginning (see I Cor. 5:1; 6:12–18; 10:8). They may indeed have been mentioned in the parts of the letter containing chapters 10—13 which have not survived. When people move into Christianity from a culture whose moral attitudes are different, it is inevitable that they carry over some of their old attitudes and revert to them at times. This is true not only of sexual attitudes but also in other areas, for example, commercial practices. Often when something new is proposed in a church, the first question asked is not whether it will advance the gospel but whether it can be paid for. Above all the books must be balanced.

While it is natural that Paul should grieve over those who have not repented, it is surprising to find him speaking of himself as humbled. (In a few translations "again" is attached to "humble" and not to "come." It is possible to understand in that way, but if so, we do not know in what Paul's previous humbling consisted.) Has his mission failed if sexual sin has not been eradicated, or if he has to use his authority to discipline rather than build up? Perhaps his opponents have pointed out those who have sinned and said that their existence proves both his gospel and his apostolic claim to be false. Yet Paul does not say he has been humbled by the Corinthians but by God. Always Paul holds his behavior before God, for God will be his judge and not the Corinthians. For ourselves it is, in the final issue, not those for whom we are pastorally responsible and who go astray who will humble us but it is God.

II Corinthians 13:1–10
Preparations for Paul's Visit

In verses 1–4 Paul explains what his presence in Corinth may mean and, therefore, in verses 5–9 summons the Corinthians to a rigorous self-examination so that when he comes he may not have to exert his authority too sternly (v. 10).

The foundation of Paul's argument is Deuteronomy 19:15, a text which was important in Jewish legal practice. It requires the testimony of at least two or three witnesses if a crime is to be proved. In our passage the "third" and "second" (visits) apparently correspond with the required "three" and "two" witnesses (this correlation is not always brought out in older translations), and Paul intends his three visits to be understood as the equivalent of three witnesses. We would normally expect the witnesses to be three different people and their testimony to refer to the same group of facts. There is, however, some evidence in Judaism that three warning visits by the same person could be regarded as equivalent to three witnesses. We would also not expect witness and judge to be the same person. Before we become too critical, we need to remember that our systems of justice have been built up through the centuries and should not without thought be read back into the first century and used to condemn its practices. (Equally we should not apply first century ideas to our modern situations.) We need also to remember that Paul as a Jew came to Corinth with higher ideas of right and wrong than the vast majority of his Gentile converts; left to themselves they might never have done anything to change the situation. He was their "father" and as such in the ancient world he had every right to step in to set right what was wrong.

Paul still has in mind the two types of sin referred to in 12:20–21. Some of those who sinned, particularly by being contentious, may even have been on Paul's side in what was going on. But if they struggle for Paul in a contentious manner, they are equally deserving of rebuke with those who oppose him.

Paul suspects the Corinthians will not take what he has to say with sufficient seriousness, for when he was face to face with them on his second visit, he seemed to be weak (10:2,10). They will now find out their error and discover he can be as strong as his letters. The real proof for that lies not in his power to work miracles or his ability to endure untold suffering but in the basic structure of his and their faith in Christ (v. 3–4): the fundamental christological paradox of the weakness of the cross and the power of the resurrection. These are not simply two temporally successive events but two sides of the same coin in which weakness and strength go together. The cross may look weak, but it

128

possesses all the strength of God (I Cor. 1:25). If this is true for Christ, it is true also for his servant Paul. He is simultaneously weak and strong since he participates in both the dying and the risen Christ (4:10; Phil. 3:10). We should again note that when Paul is driven to the wall by opposition, he does not retreat into prudential excuses but draws on the very heart of the gospel.

Paul is not thinking here of the iron hand in the velvet glove: If he has dealt gently with them up to now and they have not responded, there is steel to come! That is not the weakness of the cross. Nor is that weakness one which quietly tries to outmaneuver others and when that fails reveals its true strength. It is the weakness with which Jesus allowed men to do what they wanted with him and did not resist. Paul had accepted rebuff on his second visit. The Corinthians may have thought him a spineless creature, but he was, in fact, displaying the weakness of Christ. Already, however, he lives also in the power of the risen Christ. If character is needed, all the strength of Jesus' character is in him. If he needs to speak, Christ will speak in him (cf. 2:17). He has the mind of Christ (I Cor. 2:16; cf. 7:40) for Christ lives in him (Gal. 2:20). The Corinthians ought already to be aware of Christ's power in Paul, for it was present when he endured suffering, when the Spirit healed through him, when above all else he had preached to them and won them for Christ.

We might think that Paul ought to go on enduring rebuke, rebuff, and misunderstanding in the spirit of Jesus rather than disciplining them. Yet it is not just Paul's own position which is at stake. The sexual immorality and contentiousness within the community need to be dealt with for the sake both of its erring individuals and the good of the whole community. So Paul must show strength, though if only he himself were involved, he would not take any action. Indeed, when he has written this letter, he will probably pass through as deep a period of worry as he did after the letter referred to in 7:8. If in a pastoral situation we need to exercise discipline, then it is important that we do not do so because our own position is threatened but only in order that we may help those for whom we are responsible. We can discover whether we have been concerned primarily with our own position if when we have taken some action we keep thinking of its effect on ourselves and do not find ourselves praying for those in our care.

129

For the possible steps that Paul could have taken if he came to Corinth and found that the situation had not improved see the comment on 10:1–6.

Paul does not want to have to exercise discipline. He would rather that wrongdoers repented. So he goes on to urge them to examine themselves. He knows though that the Corinthians would like to put him to the test (v. 3; the words "proof" in v. 3, "test" in vv. 5,7 and "failed" in vv. 6,7 all come from the same Greek root). It is clearly right that those who are cared for by others should know something about them and their qualifications, but before they begin to criticize they ought to examine themselves so that they do not condemn capriciously. Self-criticism is the presupposition for all criticism of others.

If then the Corinthians are to examine themselves, along what lines should they do so? They should ask themselves if they are holding the faith (v. 5). This does not mean they should examine their intellectual beliefs or their power to move mountains and speak in tongues or their ability to stand firm under persecution. For Paul faith is primarily an attitude of trust and obedience towards God through Christ. He is therefore asking the very basic question: Are they still Christians? (This implies that it would be possible for them, once having been Christians, to cease to be such.) Clearly Paul does not anticipate that they will answer "No!" for he goes on to remind them that Christ is in them. Indeed if he had suspected they would answer "No," he would have written an entirely different letter. Yet the fact that he asks the question shows he does not have the same confidence about them as he had had in 1:24.

Paul often writes of Christians as "in Christ," only occasionally, as here, of Christ being in them (cf. Gal. 2:20; he more regularly speaks of the Spirit as in believers, for example, Rom. 8:9; I Cor. 6:19). Because we live in a much more individualistic society than Paul, we tend to look on the question "Is Christ in you?" as summoning each Christian to an individual examination. Paul, however, is more probably reminding the church in Corinth that as the body of Christ it is the temple of the Spirit and that Christ dwells in it (I Cor. 3:16). An appeal to individuals would only increase the existing divisions within the church.

130 Since Paul has called the church to self-examination, it is surprising to find him saying, "I hope you will find out that *we* have not failed." Yet if through their self-examination they discover that they no longer are holding the faith, all Paul's work

in Corinth will have come to nothing, and he will have failed. Paul has to give an answer to God for his mission work (5:10). There is then much at stake both for Paul and for them. If they meet the test, his work will stand. It will have been built with gold and silver and not hay or stubble (I Cor. 3:12). Indeed Paul cannot conceive of himself doing anything other than building like that (this is why he writes "seems to have failed"). His confidence emerges in another of those astounding parenthetical statements that he throws in from time to time, "We cannot do anything against the truth, but only for the truth." The truth here is the truth of the gospel. He will never sell the gospel short by tampering with it to make things easy for himself or to blunt its sharpness for others (4:2; 6:7; 10:11). He can therefore neither deviate in his expression of it nor moderate its consequences for the Corinthians.

This brings us back to the Corinthians, for Paul is more concerned about their possible failure than his own. He prays for their reformation (vv. 7,9), even though he himself may appear to have failed. If they meet the test of self-examination, the result will not be a holy huddle in which they tell one another how Christian they are and what deep religious feelings they have. Instead they will no longer "do wrong" but do "what is right." They will show "improvement" (v. 9). "Improvement" is a weak rendering of the underlying Greek word. It signifies their being restored or made perfect, something much more than a minor improvement. In the light of 12:20–21 Paul will be thinking of them abandoning their contentiousness and sexual immorality. He longs to hear of their godly grief and repentance (cf. 7:7–11) and will rejoice when he does so both for their sakes, because he has their true interests at heart, and for his own, because his work will not have failed.

Finally he picks up again the theme of weakness and strength and gives it a new twist. If they repent, then when he returns he will not need to exhibit strength (v. 9) or be severe (v. 10). A "strong" letter now may remove the need for a "strong" face to face encounter then. He hopes at that time to find that the Corinthians themselves are "strong." They will become this if their self-examination leads to repentance and renewal. However if his present appeal by letter is not effective, when he comes he will have to use his authority (cf. 10:8) in a way he does not wish to use it, not to build up but to discipline. Discipline is destructive and represents failure. At all costs he

131

wants to avoid it and to "build up." He uses here the same word he used in I Corinthians 14:3,4,5,12,17,26 (often translated "edify") in relation to the value of charismatic gifts. Their true use should be to build up the community. Whatever then we do in situations of criticism, either as the subjects of adverse criticism or as critics of others, we should have this and this alone as our purpose—to build up and not to tear down.

Paul desires to see the Corinthians strong. Paradoxically their strength will come through his weakness (v. 9). Here is the same thought we found in 1:3-7 and 4:12: an interchange of attributes. As Christ's weakness in death is our strengthening, so should Paul's weakness produce strength in them. When we go to help others, do we set out to emphasize primarily our strength or our weakness?

Paul and His Opponents

Difficulties of various kinds concerning ethical behavior, worship, and belief had been present in Corinth from as early as First Corinthians. It is only in Second Corinthians, however, that people appear opposed to both Paul and his views. These were not the same as those who caused the various kinds of troubles he describes in the earlier letter, but they brought about the climate in which the later opposition could grow.

Scholars have great difficulty in identifying with any precision those who opposed Paul. They have been taken to be Judaizers who wished to fasten the Jewish law on the new converts, enthusiasts who desired a wholly spiritual and charismatic faith, "divine men" who claimed to have supernatural powers, Gnostics who believed salvation came through knowledge rather than faith. Each view can find some support from what Paul writes, but it is difficult to delineate a single group in which we can simultaneously discover all the elements to which he alludes. Yet nothing suggests Paul was attacking more than one group, for he does not distinguish between groups of rivals. In the light of 11:22 we can at least say that Paul's opponents were Jewish Christians of some kind, but whether from the mother church of Jerusalem or from the Diaspora or to what extent they had been affected by the Hellenistic spirit is much less clear.

There are at least three general difficulties in their identification: (i) Paul's references to them are mainly allusions, for the original readers knew whom he meant. (ii) We have only Paul's side of the discussion and do not know how they would have described themselves or defended their position. (iii) We cannot be sure that Paul was fully informed about the situation at Corinth. He may have made the wrong criticisms or have written ambiguously in order to cover more than one possibility.

Instead of spending time identifying his opponents, it is more important to see the ways in which he combats them and their views, for we are unlikely to face exactly the same theological, moral, and ecclesiastical opponents as he did. As we have seen, his opponents were not local Christians but intruders from other churches who imparted false views on the nature of the gospel and on how to judge its true preachers. Thus at stake in chapters 10—13 has been not only the nature of the gospel but also Paul's own position.

Today Christians continually run into criticism from those outside the church, humanists, marxists, agnostics, members of other religions. Paul however was at loggerheads with those who would have hotly denied that they were outside the church. There are still Christians who denounce one another and often in shriller tones than their non-Christian contemporaries use! How then do we deal with Christians with whom we disagree, whose claim to be Christian we disallow, or who disallow our claim?

There are a number of ways in which disputes may be carried on. One side may simply and positively set out its own position indicating all its advantages or may attack the logic and impracticability of its opponents' position; or, more probably, do both at once since it is difficult in practice to separate the two. Another set of interwoven approaches is also possible—to attack the character of one's opponents and defend one's own genuineness. Often all these types of arguing appear in the same discussion.

Those who come to the final chapters of our letter with the Paul of Romans in mind are surprised to see how little rational exposition Paul gives either in defense of his own views or in rebuttal of those of his rivals. Clearly there are important intellectual differences between them, for he accuses them among other things of preaching another Jesus (11:4). It is natural that we who live after the passage of so many centuries of Christian discussion should want to pin down these differences. Paul, however, has not supplied us with enough information to do

133

this, for his method of dispute has centered on his own and his opponents' characters. It is not that he has spent overmuch time defaming them. It was sufficient to recall their self-commendation and describe them as Satanic. Almost all his discussion is taken up with his self-defense.

His character had come under attack—in relation to his economic independence and financial dealings, to an apparent difference in personal confrontation and in letter, to his lack of rhetorical skill. His position as apostle came under even more severe attack. Surprisingly, in his defense he does not detail the achievements we would list for him—his successful missions, his tremendous fight for the inclusion of Gentiles in the church on the same terms as Jews, his insight into the depths of the Christian faith and his expression of it. Only the brief reference of 12:12 touches on these achievements. Instead he tells how he suffered as he carried out his mission. Even though he recounts one moment when he was raptured into Paradise, he quickly turns it into a statement of his own weakness (12:9).

With this, his weakness, the real basis of his argument appears. His ultimate claim to be God's messenger to the Corinthians rests on the conformity of his life to that of the suffering Jesus. There have been moments, a few in our own letter, when he has failed to live like him. He has been overprickly when things have not gone the way he would have wanted, but then as the father of his converts he has behaved as any parent would when his children have come under attack. In the final issue, however, his defense rests on the fact that by and large he has not failed. He has been weak as Christ was weak on the cross, but such weakness is not failure.

We have seen that there are two basic ways of dealing with opponents, through rational argument and through attacks on character. We normally hold the first in higher regard. Why then does Paul not employ it? A politician whose position is assailed may defend it by asserting the legality of his office. Paul elsewhere defends his apostleship on this type of ground—he has seen the risen Lord (I Cor. 9:1)—and he can assume the Corinthians know this since it was to them he wrote about it. Yet legalistic claims do not mean an office is being fulfilled. God's true servant is one whose life displays the spirit of the gospel in weakness and not in glory or self-importance. By the way he has argued, Paul has lifted the genuineness of any claim to pastoral responsibility to a new and higher level. The claim to legitimacy of appointment or to orthodoxy of belief are valueless unless accompanied by a life of weakness such as we see in Jesus. How do we and those to whom we minister in pastoral care measure up to this?

II Corinthians 13:11–14
Final Greetings and Blessing

Verses 11–14 are a typical ending to a Pauline letter. Although Second Corinthians may be composed of a number of letter fragments, they are probably the original ending to 10:1 —13:10. For example, "mend your ways" picks up "improvement" in verse 9 (they are verb and noun from the same Greek root) and the exhortations there. The accompanying phrases also fit with what Paul has been saying in the preceding chapters.

These chapters are variously divided (some amalgamate vv. 12 and 13 into one verse) and rendered in different translations. Every word in general use in a language has a number of meanings. Usually the context determines the meaning to be taken, but here it is too brief to assist us. The three phrases "farewell," "mend your ways," "heed my appeal" are just single words in Greek, and each can be understood in at least two ways.

"Farewell" was at that time a customary word with which to end letters, but it also can be translated "rejoice, be happy." The tone of the preceding chapters suggests Paul's readers would not have understood it as anything other than the normal greeting. As such it contains about as much feeling as "sincerely yours." Paul softens it with "brothers."

"Mend your ways" also could be translated "may your ways be mended" with God understood as the one to do the mending or "mend one another's ways" where the emphasis is corporate rather than individual. There is a lot to be said for this last translation. Christians in those days had a less individualistic approach to their religion than do we. No matter which meaning is taken, there is no doubt Paul saw considerable room for improvement.

"Heed my appeal" could also be "exhort, encourage one

135

another," which would fit well with the third possibility for the last phrase. The Corinthians are able to assist one another in the reformation Paul desires, for they have not all become followers of his rivals.

The final two exhortations of verse 11, "agree with one another" and "live in peace," make clear the need for the corporate action we have already detected and are a necessary counter to the existing quarrelsomeness. The members of a divided church need to learn to act together.

Since they cannot do this by themselves, Paul promises that God will be there to help them. He is the God of love and peace and in situations of conflict what is needed above all is the peace and love that he alone can give.

Paul regularly concludes his letters with greetings from those who are with him when he writes. "All the saints" does not then mean that Paul sends the greetings of all Christians everywhere but only of those from where he is writing. We do not know where this was, but the messenger who took the letter would have told the Corinthians. Paul does not greet by name any of those to whom he is writing as he often does in letters; there is no need for he will soon be with them. In any case to name individuals might well have deepened the divisions in the church.

He encourages the Corinthians to greet one another with a holy kiss. This is not a deliberate attempt to counter disputatiousness, for he uses the same exhortation in other letters (Rom. 16:16; I Cor. 16:20; I Thess. 5:26). He probably expects the Corinthians to kiss one another at this point in the public reading of his letter. In the later church the kiss came to be associated with the Eucharist. Its description as "holy" eliminates any sexual aspect. It was given on the brow and shoulders, and since it was the way in which members of a family greeted one another, it would serve to remind believers that they were members of the family of God.

All Paul's letters close with some form of blessing (e.g., Rom. 16:20; I Cor. 16:23); ours is the most elaborate. It has three clauses whereas the others have only one (the grace of Christ). Why has Paul extended the blessing on this occasion? It is not a deliberate theological construction intended to teach the threefold nature of God and the relation of Father, Son, and Holy Spirit to one another. The emphasis lies on grace, love, and fellowship as three things for which Paul prays for the Corinthi-

136

ans. If Paul had been attempting a precise Trinitarian statement, he would have begun with God the Father and have used
the term "Father." Since the reference to Christ comes first, the
threefold blessing probably evolved out of the more usual single
blessing concerning the grace of Christ and is more solemn. In
using the threefold blessing, Paul (cf. I Cor. 12:4–6) did, however, help to create a problem for the later church, which it
solved with the doctrine of the Trinity.

Verse 14 is then a prayer in which three aspects of the
Christian life are highlighted. From Christ comes the grace by
which people become Christians. No virtue or accomplishment
in themselves can make them such. Behind the grace stands the
love of God from which all redemption begins and in which it
will end. Christ and God are active in creating grace and love.
Is then the Holy Spirit active in creating fellowship *(koinonia)?*
This is another word which the translations render differently.
Basically there are two ways of taking it. We may understand
it (RSV text) as Christians entering into a fellowship with one
another created for them by the Spirit; such a meaning is relevant to a divided church like Corinth. Paul is then praying for
their growth in fellowship. We may understand it (RSV margin)
as Christians participating in the Spirit. Paul would then be
praying for a deepening of their experience of the Spirit. This
would be equally appropriate to Corinth. In the end the two
meanings are not very different since to participate in the Spirit
is always to participate with other people—a corporate experience. Both meanings are relevant to the way the Corinthian
charismatics stressed the Spirit (I Cor., chaps. 12—14). It may
have been this that led Paul to add the third clause to the
blessing.

Conclusion

If chapters 10—13 were part of the "intermediate" or "painful" letter, then we know from chapters 1—9 that Paul's purpose in writing them was successful. If, as is more probable, they postdate chapters 1—9, then we have no knowledge from Paul's own letters of their effect on the Corinthian situation. There is some evidence, however, which suggests he was successful. It is almost certain he spent the last three months of his so-called third missionary journey in Europe at Corinth and from there wrote Romans. That letter shows none of the stress or strain we might have expected if his relations with the Corinthians had not been straightened out. In it (Rom. 15:26) he mentions the collection he is just about to take to Jerusalem and specifically refers to the contribution from Achaia of which Corinth was the main church. Corinth must, therefore, have cooperated with Paul in the collection. But the very survival of chapters 10—13 is itself probably decisive. Paul would not have preserved carbon or photo copies of his letter; the Corinthians must have preserved the original. Would they have preserved so trenchant a criticism of themselves if they had permanently rejected Paul? A final piece of evidence comes from the end of the first century. Clement, a leader of the church in Rome, wrote to Corinth and refers both to First Corinthians (I Clement 47:1) and to Paul himself as an example whom the Corinthians would respect (I Clement 5:5-7). He would hardly have done this unless Paul and his writings were held in honor in Corinth. We may then assume that Paul's pleas were successful and that when he came to Corinth he did not have to tear down but was able to build up.

Bibliography

1. For further study

BARRETT, C. K. *The Second Epistle to the Corinthians* (London: A & C Black, 1973).

BRUCE, F. F., ed. *I & II Corinthians*. NEW CENTURY BIBLE (London: Marshall, Morgan & Scott, 1971).

BULTMANN, RUDOLF. *The Second Letter to the Corinthians* (Minneapolis: Augsburg, 1985).

FILSON, F. V. *The Second Epistle to the Corinthians*, Introduction and Exegesis; James Reid, Exposition in Interpreter's Bible (New York & Nashville: Abingdon Press, 1953), Vol. 10, 263–425.

FURNISH, V. P. *II Corinthians*. THE ANCHOR BIBLE (New York: Doubleday, 1984).

HANSON, R.P.C. *The Second Epistle to the Corinthians*. TORCH BIBLE COMMENTARIES (London: S.C.M. Press, 1967).

HERING, J. *The Second Epistle of St. Paul to the Corinthians*, A. W. Heathcote and P. J. Allcock, Eng. trans. (London: Epworth Press, 1967).

HUGHES, P. E. *Paul's Second Epistle to the Corinthians*. THE NEW INTERNATIONAL COMMENTARY ON THE NEW TESTAMENT (Grand Rapids: Eerdmans, 1962).

MARTIN, R.P. *2 Corinthians*. WORD BIBLICAL COMMENTARY 40 (Waco: Word Books, 1986).

PLUMMER, A. *The Second Epistle of St. Paul to the Corinthians*. THE INTERNATIONAL CRITICAL COMMENTARY (Edinburgh: T. & T. Clark, 1915).

STRACHAN, R. H. *The Second Epistle of Paul to the Corinthians*. THE MOFFATT NEW TESTAMENT COMMENTARY (London: Hodder and Stoughton, 1935).

THRALL, M.E. *The First and Second Letters of Paul to the Corinthians*. CAMBRIDGE BIBLE COMMENTARY (Cambridge: Cambridge University Press, 1965).

On the City of Corinth see

MURPHY-O'CONNOR, J. *St. Paul's Corinth: Texts and Archaeology* (Wilmington, Del.: Michael Glazier, 1983).

2. Literature cited

DENNEY, JAMES. The Second Epistle to the Corinthians, in W. Robertson Nicoll, ed., *The Expositor's Bible* (London: Hodder and

141

Stoughton, 1894; Hartford: The S. S. Scranton Company, N.D. [V, 716—809]).

HENNECKE, Edgar, in *New Testament Apocrypha,* Vol. 2, Wilhelm Schneemelcher, ed. Eng. trans. by Ernest Best and others; R. McL. Wilson, Eng. ed. (Philadelphia: Westminster Press, 1965).

HERBERT, GEORGE. *The Country Parson.* Edited with Introduction by John N. Wall, Jr. (New York: Paulist Press, 1981).